So
You Want
to Know About
Economics

Roopa Pai has written over twenty books for children, covering the gamut from fantasy to popular science to philosophy. She combines three other loves—history, young people, and her hometown Bangalore—in her job as a tour guide with heritage walks and tours company, BangaloreWalks. Her bestselling *The Gita For Children* won the Crossword Popular Award for Children's Writing in 2016.

Mohit Suneja started his life as an artist from a young age when he drew portraits and copied action figures from comic books. He followed his passion and trained at the College of Art, New Delhi where he later went on to teach as a professor of Visual Communication. He has since worked in many roles in many industries and created everything from book covers to wall paintings. Today, Mohit is set to travel at the speed of his imagination trying to create a better world through his art.

So
You Want
to Know About
Economics

ROOPA PAI

Illustrated by Mohit Suneja

RED TURTLE
RUPA

Published by
Rupa Publications India Pvt. Ltd 2017
7/16, Ansari Road, Daryaganj
New Delhi 110002

Sales centres:
Allahabad Bengaluru Chennai
Hyderabad Jaipur Kathmandu
Kolkata Mumbai

ISBN: 978-81-291-4519-2

Seventh impression 2018

10 9 8 7

The moral right of the author has been asserted.

Printed at Rakmo Press Pvt. Ltd, New Delhi

For Dhwani Yagnaraman and Inika Prasad,
future economists and overall rockstars,
with many thanks for test-driving this book.

CONTENTS

INTRODUCTION

WHY SHOULD WE TALK ABOUT ECONOMICS?

Here's an idea. Pick up a notebook and pen, walk to the nearest adult, and with your most earnest face (practice in front of the mirror first), tell them you are conducting a Very Important survey for a school project. There are only two questions, so would they please give you five minutes of their time? If you live with more or less reasonable people, they will most likely agree.

When your unsuspecting victim has settled down, ask her your first question:

'What is your opinion of Economics as a subject?'

The person you are interviewing will most likely look distinctly traumatised by the question. Then she will perhaps respond in one of the following ways.

▶ 'Absolutely. The. Most. Mind-numbingly. Boring. Subject. On. Earth!'

▶ 'You'd have to be a math genius to even begin to understand what the subject is about. I'm not.'

▶ 'I passed with decent marks, but if you asked me what Economics taught me, I don't quite, erm, know.'

▶ 'No opinion at all. I've never studied it, and never been tempted to. Can I go now? I have to pee.'

Pushing on ruthlessly, ask the second question:

'What do you think about when you think about Economics?'

People who have never studied the subject will be wonderfully vague. 'It's about money, right? About budgets—how a country divides the money it has? About GDP and stocks and shares and... uh, stuff to do with the Reserve Bank and the Finance Minister and taxes... and... oh all right, all *right*, I admit it, I don't think about Economics at *all*. Please don't judge me.'

People who *have* studied the subject, on the other hand, will clear their throats, sit up straighter, and proceed to throw random words and phrases at you. 'It's about, you know, markets and things. Supply, demand, price elasticity, externalities, cost-benefit, scarcity, resources, exchange rates, maximising utility, protectionism, globalisation, and all of them, of course, *ceteris paribus...*' When they finally catch your glassy-eyed expression, they will turn up their noses and say, 'See, it's Very Complicated. Difficult to explain. You wouldn't understand it.'

Only a few people—a rare species but they do exist—will smile beatifically when you ask them these questions. They will lean forward in their seats, faces animated, eyes sparkling, and tell you that Economics is the most exciting subject in the world. Over the next half hour, pinning you to your seat with their fire-and-brimstone eyes, they will tell you why they think so. This is what they might say:

1. Economics is important because it is really the study of how the world thinks and works! See, economists are really psychologists in disguise—they have looked into the deepest, darkest recesses of the human heart and discovered that all of us are essentially selfish beings at the core. But if every person is doing selfish things that only benefit him or her, how come society is doing more or less okay? Economists believe they have the answer to that Big Question, and they spend their lives figuring out how to arrange things in the world so that society benefits while people go on doing their selfish things.

2. Economists are really superheroes fighting for a fairer world! One of their lives' Big Challenges is to figure out the best ways to share the world's limited resources (like minerals, metals, oil, human labour, time, energy or money) amongst people who have unlimited needs, in ways that are as moral and ethical as possible. They constantly obsess over how to make things somewhat equitable for everyone—the rich and the poor, developed countries and developing countries, the healthy and the sick, and the old and the young, so that both sides benefit. They look at every problem from more than one point of view, and then they present all the different views, so that people can make the right choice for themselves.*

---

*Economists are so particular about looking at every problem from all sides that it often feels like they never have a firm opinion on anything. That can get pretty frustrating when you are asking them for advice. Harry Truman, the 33rd President of the United States, once famously requested to be sent a 'one-armed economist', because he was so tired of hearing every economist say, 'On the one hand, this,' and 'On the other hand, that'.

3. Economists are closet environmentalists. Just like environmentalists, they are constantly trying to understand how we, the 7 billion people that inhabit this planet, can get the most out of what the universe gives us for free—sunlit skies, clean air, flowing rivers, lush forests—without mindlessly destroying it and ruining things for ourselves. The two groups have very different ideas on how to make this happen, though.

4. Economists are wizards who make magical things happen with numbers. They have shown, time and again, that when, say, a billion people work together, the sum of their individual efforts is far greater than what it is supposed to be.

5. And by the way, if someone told you they didn't think about Economics at all, they don't know what they're talking about, because *everyone* is thinking Economics *all* the time, even if they don't realize it. Every time you go into a supermarket and find your favourite breakfast cereal, you are benefiting from the Economics of a free market, which makes sure that everything the consumer wants (and some stuff that she doesn't even know she wants!) is available easily to her. Every time you scarf down a dosa at your local South Indian café, you are helping the economy of your neighbourhood grow. Every time you pay for a plastic bag in a store because you neglected to bring your own from home, you are participating in the fight for a cleaner, less toxic world (who do you think came up with the idea to have people pay for plastic bags so that they eventually use less of

them? An economist!). So there!

By now, you are convinced that your manic-eyed interviewee is either wilfully exaggerating or has a couple of screws loose. But admit it, either way, your interest has been piqued.

So stick around and listen in while we talk about Economics. I'm betting you'll be glad you did.

THE WORLD BEFORE ECONOMICS

Let's begin with a quick flashback to 2 million years ago, when the first human (or maybe she was the fifty-ninth) walked jauntily out of her cave, swinging a stick she had just found. It was a beautiful day, and our human was feeling chuffed—as far as she knew, she was the only creature in the world that walked on two legs, plus she had an interesting-looking stick!

Her happy state of mind didn't last, however. Ten minutes later, she ran into Another Human. One part of her mind conceded that it might be fun to have a companion, but the other part was already looking longingly at the smooth flat stones that he was playing with. Oh, she wanted those stones, and she knew only one way of getting them. She raised her stick to knock He-Human on the head, when she noticed that he was looking at her stick with the same moony expression.

She-Human's brain went into overdrive as a Big Idea began to form. Maybe there was another way to do this.

'Oonga, oonga?' said She-Human, extending the stick.

'Yabba-Dabba-Doo!' exulted He-Human, happily handing over his stones.

Grinning like loons, She- and He-Human walked off into the sunset, arms around each other's shoulders—the first-ever trade had been made!

Since that historic moment, humans haven't stopped trading with each other. Shiny beads for cloth, cows for cooking pots, gold for pepper, carbon emissions for clean air—substitute anything for anything on either side of the equation and it is likely that the two have been traded at some time, in some form, at some price or the other.

But why are we jabbering about trade here? Because contrary to popular belief, it is trade that makes the world go round, not money! Money is just what is used to conduct a trade. See? You learn something new everyday!

FOLLOW THE MONEY

So we've established that trade is the root of all Economics. And we know that money is the root of all trade i.e., Pretty Darn Important to this book. So let's go off and find out a little more about it, shall we?

First off, what is money? It is what we use to conduct trade in the modern world. Serious, well-informed Economics experts define it as 'any item that is generally accepted as payment for goods and repayment of debts.' Meh. You knew that.

What about the purpose and function of money? As someone put it succinctly:

Money's a matter of functions four,
A Medium, a Measure, a Standard, a Store.

Erm, say what?

See, it works like this. Money is:

▸ **A great MEDIUM of exchange:** Why? Because it's light, small and everyone will happily accept it in return for what they are selling to you or doing for you. For instance, if you said to your friend (do NOT try this at home): 'Hey, can you do my math assignment for me? I will pay you 50 bucks', it is more likely that he

Follow the money

Let's swap! (since forever)
You like my stick! I like your stones.

Proper metal coins
(2500 years ago, India, China, Lydia)
So that's what the Emperor looks like!

✳ *Money* ✳
can't buy you
happiness

(Yeah, right!)

Leather money
(2000 years ago, China) Pretty cool!
Now if we could make the same thing
using paper, and somewhat smaller.

Paper money *(1300 years ago, China)*
An idea whose time has not come.
Black to coins, chop, chop!

ttle and grain (*10,000 years ago*)
ree bushels of wheat or
ake my goat elsewhere.

Cowrie shells (*3500 years ago, India, Africa, China*)
Fine if you live by the seaside, but...

But it can do a ton of other Cool stuff

Bronze and copper cowrie shells
(*3000 years ago, China*)
Seriously? Now my wallet's way, way heavier!

Paper money returns
(*1661 CE*) Sweden issues
the first European 'banknote'.

Plastic money (*1958*)
Wallets get even lighter
with Bank of America's
'credit card'.

Invisible money (*now*)
'Dad, I just ordered an
elephant online!'

will say yes, than if you had said, 'If you do my math assignment for me, I will give you my new socks (which my grandmom bought for me and I absolutely hate), a bar of chocolate (that has been sitting around in the fridge forever), a big bear hug (see how much I love you?).'

Also, it's more convenient to carry money in your pocket than to cart a bunch of frisky goats to barter at the mall every time you go shopping.

▶ **A MEASURE of value**: Just like we have standard units to measure distance, time, weight, and temperature, 'money' is the standard unit we use to measure the 'value' of something. The more money you pay for something, the greater its 'value'.

But what we think of as 'real money' is not that different in look and feel to 'Monopoly money' (case in point: the new ₹2000 note). So what makes real money real? The fact that a country's government says it is! Within that country, these government-approved pieces of coloured paper can be used legally in exchange for 'goods' like pizza and 'services' like bus-rides.

▶ **A STANDARD of deferred* payment**: In plain English, that means money is an accepted way to pay off a loan, i.e., pay someone back tomorrow for money they lent you today. If a friend lent you 100 rupees today so that you could pitch in your share for another friend's birthday gift, she will always be happy to accept 100 rupees from you tomorrow as repayment of her loan

---

*'to defer' means 'to put off until later'

to you. She may be less happy to accept a book or a bunch of flowers as repayment, even if you say they cost *exactly* the same amount.

‣ **A STORE of value:** Remember the time you squirreled away the chocolate you got at Diwali just so that you could bring it out after your sibling had run through his share? What you had done was to create a 'store of value', whose 'value' was the expression on your sibling's face when he discovered your treachery. You couldn't have done the squirreling away with, say, strawberries, because they would spoil if you kept them too long. Money is like chocolate—it doesn't spoil (although it might be less valuable the longer you keep it, because of something called inflation, which we will talk about on page 92). So if you salt away your pocket money instead of wasting it on things that you can arm-twist your parents into paying for, you would have created another store of value to torture your sibling with. (Also, if you had put your money into a bank, instead of just stuffing it into your underwear drawer, you would have created an even *larger* store of value because of something called **interest** which a bank would pay you. We'll talk about this in more detail on page 138.) The danger of not putting your money in a bank is that when something like **demonetisation** comes along (it happens rarely, but it does happen, as we found out in November 2016), that money turns instantly into nothing more than coloured pieces of paper that have no value. (We'll talk a little more about that on page 56.)

OKAY, WE'VE GOT MONEY FIGGERED OUT.
CAN WE GET TO ECONOMICS ALREADY?

Not so fast! You see, Economics, as we understand it today, is a fairly new idea, and to understand why someone thought it up, we need to know what went before. 'Economics', as a branch of study, didn't even exist 250 years ago. Coming to think of it, neither did electricity, sliced bread, plastic, selfies, or the United States of America. Why, there weren't even any *other* countries, or, more accurately, 'nation-states', in those days.

Nation-state? Wozzat?

To answer that question, we have to time-travel back to the fifteenth century. At that time, if you took any region of the known world, it was basically a patchwork of kingdoms or tribal societies, some small, some large, with loosely-defined borders. Even in large kingdoms, the king or emperor rarely had absolute control. It worked like this—a powerful king would conquer a small neighbouring kingdom, and would then allow the defeated king to continue ruling his kingdom, with the old rules and laws. The only conditions? The smaller king paid the more powerful one a yearly tribute of a large amount of money, and maintained an army to fight off the big guy's enemies.

Overall, a win-lose situation was turned into a win-(sort-of)-win situation. The big king got more money into his treasury and left the headache of fighting off enemies in that region to someone else, and the smaller king got to stay king.

What about the common people? Often, they didn't even know that they had been conquered. They lived in their faraway villages, worked on their farms or their weaving looms or potter's wheels, rarely travelled, and spent their spare time worrying about how they were going to pay their taxes to their greedy landlords and still feed their families. Without newspapers, television or the Internet, they very rarely knew what their king even looked like. Needless to say, they didn't feel any loyalty to him or to their 'country'.

As you can see, it was all a bit vague on every side. To add to the confusion, things were constantly shifting and changing. For instance, a couple of months after he had been conquered, the smaller king would declare his independence and refuse to pay the yearly tribute. He would sneakily get into alliances with the big king's enemies and plan attacks on the big king. Or maybe the big king would get swallowed up by a bigger one, and the small king would only realize this some six months later when a trader from the capital happened to be passing through his kingdom and brought the news.

Things may have proceeded indefinitely in this manner if it hadn't been for Europe. In the fourteenth century, a new and exciting energy had begun to sweep across Europe as it shook off a dull and dreary period of its history, now called the Dark Ages. The rumble began in Italy, but soon spread across the continent. People who had blindly followed the rules laid down by priests and kings and rarely thought about things for themselves began to question everything. These new 'rebels' were curious about all kinds of stuff: How do things work? Does the Bible really say what the priests say it says? Is there anything I can build to make my work easier?

They were also full of a grand sense of adventure and hope. Surely there is more to the world than my little village? Surely not everyone in the world has to grow crops or make pots—what if I want to paint, or write, or play my lute, and make a living that way? Surely a man has it in his power to fashion his own destiny?

People began to experiment with art, science, politics, literature, architecture, music and philosophy. The outpouring of creativity felt like a revival of the intelligence and energy of mankind itself. The invention of the printing press in 1440 by German innovator Johannes Gutenberg helped these revolutionary ideas spread quickly, encouraging more people to think and build and paint and write. No wonder the period is now called the Renaissance ('rebirth' in French).

Kings and queens began thinking out of the box, too. Towards the middle of the fifteenth century, Henry VII in England and King Ferdinand and Queen Isabella in Spain emerged as the builders of the first 'nation-states'— kingdoms where the rulers (and not a random bunch of chieftains) held all the power, where all the people of the kingdom followed the same set of rules and laws and paid the same taxes, and where everyone felt they were part of one big (if not-always-happy) family.

The nation-state was a pretty neat idea. OR was it?

Well, it was certainly a better idea than what had gone before, but like every other idea, this one too had its good and not-so-good bits.

The good bits

- With only one super boss (the king or queen), the day-to-day working of the kingdom became more organized.
- With one set of laws for the entire kingdom, people felt that things were generally fairer than before. Earlier, if you were a peasant unlucky enough to have a bad landlord, you were destined to live a far more miserable life than someone with a kinder one, but now who your landlord was didn't matter as much.
- With soldiers from the super boss' army guarding the borders of the kingdom, people felt safer. Now any wars that happened would happen with people *outside* the kingdom, not inside it.
- Within the clearly-defined boundary of the kingdom, merchants and traders could travel freely, selling their wares, knowing they wouldn't be stopped at a dozen borders and made to pay a dozen tolls as they went about their business. Plus, the same taxes applied everywhere, which made it easier for them to fix one single price for their goods throughout the kingdom.
- Everyone felt like they belonged together, and were part of something glorious that was bigger than themselves—a country, a flag, a people!

The bad bits

- Absolute power often went absolutely to the ruler's head. Very often, with no one to challenge him, the ruler focused only on giving himself and his friends a good time, and didn't give a fig for the people.

- Obviously, the laws that the king made were cleverly designed to make him and his friends (the rich people) richer, which meant the poor became poorer. In the earlier model, if you had had a good landlord, you could have had a decent life, now, if you had a bad king, you had no hope at all.

- As merchants prospered, they paid more taxes into the king's treasury, and became more and more chummy with the king. The poor peasants, who toiled so hard each day in the fields to produce food to fill the merchants' bellies, completely fell off the king's radar. Soon, merchants became so powerful that the only laws that were being made were ones that helped their cause.

- The not-so-nice part about everyone feeling like they were a band of brothers—'All for one and one for all' and such—was that, now, everyone else was 'Them', the outsider, the other, the enemy. Sure, it helped to unite the people of that nation-state, but it also helped them believe that anyone who did not belong to this 'family' deserved the worst kind of violence and exploitation. Not fun.

A SHORT BUT SPICY DETOUR

Figured out nation-states? Now let's talk about spices. Spices? Yes, yes, this book is about Economics, not spices. But spices are the, erm, spice of life. And important to our Economics story, too. You will see why as we go along.

Right then. We are still in the fifteenth century, at a time when spices, especially pepper, were worth their weight in gold in Europe (Why? Because when you used a lot of it, it masked the smell and taste of rotting meat. This was before refrigerators were invented, remember! Ugh!).

In the beginning, it was fleets of Arabian dhows that carried spices from the east—the Maluku Islands in Indonesia, Sri Lanka, the Indian peninsula—to Europe, first by sea to Egypt, then up the Nile and the Mediterranean Sea to somewhere in today's Syria, and finally by land to Constantinople (today's Istanbul), the gateway to Europe. Few Europeans knew exactly where these spices came from— the Arabs guarded their secret closely—and that made them (the Europeans) desire these exotic thingummijigs even more.

The Arabs merrily fleeced the Europeans until 1453, when Constantinople was captured by the Ottoman Turks and the land route into Europe was shut off. Europe suffered and smarted without its beloved spices, until the rulers of Spain and Portugal decided it was time a different route to the east was found. The world was round, the open sea lapped at their coasts, and adventurous sailors with stars in their eyes were a dime a dozen. Equip them with ships and men, and surely they would find their way to those fabulous eastern lands where gold, it was whispered, was brought up to the surface by hard-working gold-digging ants?

So off they went, these doughty explorers. The first to go, in 1492 CE, was Christopher Columbus of Spain, who sailed forth with the blessings of the same King Ferdinand and Queen Isabella whom we talked about earlier. He went west, bumped into two huge continents no one knew existed, and brought back not spices but strange-looking vegetables that we know today as tomatoes and potatoes and chillies, and the divine *Theobroma cacao*, food of the gods, otherwise known as the cocoa bean, the progenitor of chocolate.

In 1497, the Portuguese seaman Vasco da Gama sensibly went south along the west coast of Africa, did a hairpin bend at the Cape of Good Hope, and eventually reached Mozambique, where Kutchi sailor (Kutch is a part of Gujarat today) Kanji Malam is believed to have shown him the way to the spice garden of the world, i.e., the Malabar coast.

A new gateway to the east was now open for Europe to pour through, and the world would never be the same again.

A REVOLUTIONARY NEW BUSINESS IDEA CALLED MERCANTILISM (A.K.A. 'HOW TO GROW RICH THROUGH LOOT AND PLUNDER')

We are now in the sixteenth century. Europe's new nation-states, their powerful rulers, and their prosperous, influential merchants are doing very nicely, thank you. Now that routes to new faraway lands that are full of gold and silk and calico and spices and vulnerable, unsuspecting natives have been discovered, an audacious and disruptive new way to do business begins to take root.

The main points of this idea—Mercantilism—went something like this:

▸ Woohoo! Some of us Europeans are super-powerful! Now to get super-rich!
▸ You get super-rich by having lots of gold. Okay, silver's not too bad, either.
▸ There are *tons* of both in South and Central America
▸ One way to lay our paws on that yummy bullion* is to sell stuff from our countries to the Americans and make them pay for it in gold and silver. Sure, we can mine our own gold, but that's too much work, plus all the gold in our country is ours anyway. The point is to get *other* people's gold.
▸ We use American gold to pay for voyages to other foreign lands—India, China, the Near East, the Far East—and get *their* gold by selling them more of our stuff.
▸ When we fill our ships with our stuff and take it to

---

*Gold and silver in the form of ingots and bars rather than coins.

sell in foreign lands, we should be careful not to spend too much of our gold to buy their stuff; we should try and pay for it in some other way. There should *always* be more gold coming into the country than going out, because the only way to get richer is by making someone else poorer.

▶ Foreigners in general are way less smart, way less cool, and way less important than us, but even they will smell a rat if we keep taking their gold without giving them any in return. The best way to deal with this is to conquer them. Then we can loot and plunder them and their land legally.

- **Afterthought 1**: Oh, we can also make them our slaves—and pay them peanuts!

- **Afterthought 2**: Oh, oh, we can also buy their raw materials—their cotton, metals, leather—for really, really cheap (hey, at least we're not taking it for free!), then take it back to our own countries, turn them into finished goods (because we are *so* much better than them at manufacturing) and—get this!—sell it right back to them, and get *more* gold out of them!

- **Afterthought 3**: While we are at it, we should whip our own countrymen into shape too. We should make them work like dogs in mines, in unsanitary little sweatshops, on looms. We should pay them very little, give them no healthcare, and take their children out of school and put them to work. That way, we can produce even more finished goods to sell to those poor foreign suckers, and earn *even* more gold!

As ideas went, Mercantilism was a brilliant one for European rulers and their cronies—ministers, nobles, landowners, and merchants who traded with foreign lands—and it made Europe very, very rich.

Obviously, however, it was a terrible idea as far as the colonies (the poor foreign suckers conquered by Europe) were concerned. Why, even the non-merchants and non-nobles of Europe were not exactly loving it (refer Afterthought 3 to see why).

Clearly, the people who did *not* love the idea were in a huge majority compared to the ones that did. Which is why it is so surprising that mercantilism was considered the *only* way to do business for some 200 years, right until the end of the eighteenth century!

HERE IT COMES—THE E WORD!

As we have seen, way more people hated Mercantilism than loved it. But the reason it eventually fell by the wayside because, in the long run, it turned out to be a bad idea for *everyone*, even for the people who loved it. The guy who called out all its flaws and poked lots and lots of holes in it was a British academic and philosopher called Adam Smith. He didn't stop there either; he went on to propose a new and different idea that was not only a much better way of doing business but also benefited many more people.

In 1776 CE, Adam Smith put his thoughts down in a fat book with a very long name that we needn't concern ourselves with. All we need to know is its short name:

The Wealth of Nations. It was the modern world's very first book on—here it comes now, the word you've all so eagerly been waiting for—Economics*!

Smith firmly believed that Mercantilism was a completely flawed idea. If there had been an argument between the mercantilists and Smith, it might have gone something like this.

Mercantilists: We need to get more and more gold into the country, because the amount of gold in a country's treasury is the only measure of how much wealth the country has.

Adam Smith: Hogwash! The true measure of a country's wealth is its people, and the things they can grow or make or produce through their hard work. Just because you have more gold doesn't mean you are richer. You've got to use the gold to produce something, or to get someone to produce something for you, or to take a holiday to the Cornish coast. Gold is only useful when it is, well, used!

*At least, that's what most of the world thinks. We in India know better. Our home-grown 'book' on Economics was written almost 2000 years before Adam Smith's, in Sanskrit, by a brilliant scholar and kingmaker called Chanakya Kautilya. The book was called the *Arthashastra*, which is Sanskrit for 'The Science of Wealth'. Ta-da! Unlike Smith's book, the *Arthashastra* wasn't only about Economics, though. There were sections on politics, marriage laws, crime and punishment, government, ethics, and trade, and on the duties and obligations of a king. That's why its title is often translated as 'The Science of Politics'.

Mercantilists: We should only sell our stuff to other people. We should not buy too much from them, especially if we know how to make it ourselves. Yes, even if their stuff is better or cheaper.

Adam Smith: Balderdash! It is only through selling AND buying that wealth is created. Look at all the civilisations that flourished before us—Egypt, Greece, Rome, Mesopotamia, China, India—they didn't do business with the world using stupid ideas like these. They freely traded their stuff for other people's stuff, and THAT's how they grew rich, not by looting and plundering like you guys.

Mercantilists: There is only so much wealth in the world, so the only way we can get rich is by making someone else poor.

Adam Smith: Tommyrot! Wealth is not static, it can be created! Getting rich at someone else's expense is not only immoral, it's imbecilic! Both sellers and buyers can become rich if they trade sensibly with each other—it's only when everyone benefits that trade even makes sense!

Yup, he used a lot of colourful words to call out the stupidity of the mercantilists, but Smith's arguments were clearly sound. It explains why, a few years after *The Wealth of Nations* was published, England began to sidle slowly away from mercantilism towards Adam Smith's brand-new idea for a very different way of doing business.

400 YEARS AGO, THE ANSWER TO THE QUESTION 'WHICH IS THE WORLD'S RICHEST COUNTRY?' WAS 'INDIA!'

Yes! In the sixteenth century, when the Mughals ruled, India's GDP (**Gross Domestic Product**, or the total value of the things manufactured and produced by India in a year) was estimated to be about a quarter of the *entire world's GDP*! Or let's put it this way: in the year 1600, the annual revenue of *just* Emperor Akbar's treasury was £17.5 million* (even though large chunks of India weren't part of his kingdom); 200 years later, the entire treasury of Great Britain could not match that—its annual revenue was only £16 million.

Wow. How did we get there? Well, through many, many centuries of 'economic activities'—farming, herding, mining, manufacturing, spinning, weaving, metal-working, craft-skill-building and trading furiously and continuously with the world. And what happened to us after that, that we fell

---

*This didn't mean that the average Indian's pockets were overflowing with wealth, though. There is often no correlation between how much money is in the national treasury to how rich (or poor) the people of the nation are. You see, it isn't enough for the wealth to be there, it is how it is shared that matters. 'Distribution of wealth' is a tricky thing, because of human selfishness and greed.

off the rich countries list so dramatically?

Here's a brief history of the Economics of India, not only until the Europeans came in (when things were dandy), but also after they came in (and things went south).

When did the people of what we know today as India begin to indulge in 'economic activities'? Who knows? All the information we have about economic activities only begins with the Indus Valley Civilisation, one of the oldest civilisations in the world.

2400 BCE: The Indus Valley people lived in cities built beside mighty rivers in today's Pakistan and India (mainly Gujarat), and traded copper, different kinds of hardwoods, ivory, pearls, lapis lazuli and gold, mainly with the people of the other ancient civilisation of Mesopotamia.

In the sixth century BCE, over a thousand years after the people of the Indus Valley mysteriously disappeared, coins were minted in India for the first time. By this time, the port of Bharuch in Gujarat was well-known in Arabia and Egypt, and even as far afield as Europe. Traders from these places sailed to Bharuch not only to buy Indian goods, but also eager for luxury goods from the Far East. Because ships from the Far East docked at Bharuch too!

In the third century BCE, the Mauryan empire took over and united almost all of the land that we know today as India under one kingdom. It was then  that the Indian economy really began to take off. Without having to worry about stuff like going through unfriendly kingdoms, different currencies, different weights and measures, and the headache of paying taxes at every border, traders roamed freely across the land with their goods, along well-guarded roads that the king had constructed expressly for this purpose.

Around the time when BCE was changing into CE, and Augustus Caesar ruled at the head of the Roman Empire, the south Indian peninsula became the hub of Indian overseas trade. With the open sea calling from three sides, and no shortage of expert sailors and shipbuilders in the Tamil kingdoms of the Pandyas and the Cheras, south Indian merchants carried on a flourishing trade with West Asia. After Augustus conquered Egypt and captured the Arabian sea trade in 30 BCE, these merchants began trading directly with the mighty Roman Empire itself! They traded mainly in pepper, cotton cloth, silk yarn, indigo and gems, in exchange for lots and lots of gold.

By the ninth century, the Chola dynasty, also of Tamil Nadu, had become the masters not only of most of southern India but parts of southeast Asia. Chola trade with the Srivijaya Empire of Sumatra and the T'ang dynasty of  China—Chinese junks were a common sight at ports on the Malabar and Coramandel coasts—was as brisk and profitable as that with the Abbasid Caliphate of Baghdad. In fact, because of their location in the southern peninsula between the eastern and western seas, the Cholas helped to introduce China to the rest of the world as a trading partner.

In the fourteenth century, under the Vijayanagara Empire, trade by sea only got bigger and better. From its 300-odd ports on the coasts of the Arabian Sea and the Bay of Bengal,  where traders of many nationalities had come to live and prosper, state-of-the-art ships laden with calico, muslin, metals, pepper, ginger, cardamom, cinnamon, pearls, and porcelain sailed out to Mecca and Aden, Burma and China (China was particularly eager for our ivory and rhino horn).

By the time the Mughals came to rule us **in the sixteenth century**, India was a flourishing world economy, the second largest in the world. The port of Surat, much patronised by the Mughals, was renowned across the world for its exports of silk and diamonds, and considered one of the greatest trading cities of the world, on par with Venice and Beijing. In the year 1700, Emperor Aurangazeb reported an annual revenue of £100 million!

And then came the fall.

The Mughals themselves were responsible for the first phase of the fall. After Aurangzeb's death in 1707, the empire was ruled by a series of weak emperors for a dozen years. By the time Muhammad Shah I came to the throne in 1719, the Mughals were very much in decline.

Muhammad Shah was a great patron of the arts but, sadly, an inefficient and neglectful administrator. The death blow to the Mughal Empire came in the form of an invasion by Nader Shah of Persia in 1739. The Battle of Karnal, fought between Shah and Shah, was won by the invading Shah in less than three hours! Riding triumphantly into Delhi, Nader Shah proceeded to sack and loot it with abandon. Neither the city, nor the Mughals, recovered from that onslaught.

But it was the second phase of the fall that really destroyed the Indian economy.

In 1757, a new and powerful force, very different from anything India had seen before, began to make its presence felt. It all started innocuously enough. In Calcutta, British traders of the East India Company (which had its own well-equipped, well-trained army), helped Mir Jafar, the rebel commander of Nawab Siraj-ud-daulah of Bengal, win a battle against his king. We now know this landmark battle as the Battle of Plassey. In return, the grateful Mir Jafar gave the traders a swathe of land to rule. This had never happened before—usually, the traders' reward for helping someone win was money, or exclusive trading rights in the kingdom, or increased influence with the new king.

The British traders soon discovered that this new gig was brilliant—they did not have to sell anything to earn money now, they just collected taxes from people they ruled. And they could use that money to buy things from those same people, and never spend their gold at all!

Needless to say, they wanted more. Over the next 100 years, the East India Company managed to become India's biggest 'landlord'. During the same time period, something that we now call the 'Industrial Revolution' had begun in England. Machines were being invented that did all kinds of work way quicker, more accurately, and more efficiently than individual people could. The machines were hungry for raw material—cotton, iron, silk, indigo. And India—large, bountiful India, full of people who could be put to work, and rich with fertile fields and minerals—became the hand that fed the mouth of the mechanical beast.

Suddenly, India, a land of skilled workers which had always exported expensive finished goods (cloth, jewellery, handicraft) to the world and got gold and silver in return, was exporting cheap raw material and getting expensive finished goods in return instead. Her fields were being used to grow things that could not be eaten—cotton, jute, indigo, opium—instead of grain to fill her own people's bellies. Her farmers were forced to pay huge taxes, often with their own personal store of food grain, even when the monsoons failed, or they faced severe punishment.* Briskly-produced bales of inexpensive machine-made British cloth pushed more expensive home-spun khadi out of the market. This happened in other fields, too, with machine-made products replacing hand-made products, and turning artisans and craftspeople into beggars. Devastating famines broke out, killing tens of thousands of people.

By the time the British left, in 1947, India's share of the world's GDP had slipped from 22.6 per cent (in 1700) to a paltry 3.8 per cent! Since then, in less than seventy years, we have clawed our way back up the 'share of GDP' ladder. We are now the world's seventh-largest economy. Yes, even though we think of India as a poor country, we have plenty to be proud about!

LEARN THE LINGO

Zero-sum Game

Does someone always have to lose for someone else to win, or is it possible for both sides to win? Does trade have

---

*The 2001 blockbuster Bollywood film *Lagaan*, the Hindi word for tax, is a period film set against this very backdrop.

to be a win-lose game, like Mercantilism was, or could it become a win-win game, where both sides benefit? In other words, is trade a zero-sum game? Let's try and understand this with an example.

It's your birthday. Your parents have ordered your favourite flavour of cake for your party. You have six friends coming. The easiest way to divide the cake into equal pieces is to cut it first into quarters, and then into eighths, making eight equal pieces. But there are only seven of you, and it is a bit tricky to divide the cake into seven equal pieces. Your friends decide that because it is YOUR birthday, you get two pieces (i.e., 2/8ths of the whole cake), while each of them gets 1/8th of the cake. In the end, each of them gets a little less than what they could have if the division had been equal, and you get a lot more.

You dig in a little guiltily. What you would have liked is for each of your six friends to get their 1/7ths of the cake (what they fairly deserve), using up 6/7ths of the cake, while you still got your 2/8ths (a little more than everyone else, because it is your special day). But that is a mathematical impossibility since there is only one cake ($6/7 + 2/8 > 1$). This kind of situation, where, because there is a limited amount of something, someone has to 'lose' (or get less of something) for someone else to 'win' (or get more of something) is called a zero-sum game. All zero-sum games are therefore 'win-lose' games.

The mercantilists believed that wealth was a zero-sum game—there was a limited amount of wealth in the world, and to 'win', you needed to grab someone else's wealth, which would make that someone else 'lose'. Adam Smith and other like-minded economists begged to disagree. They believed that the amount of wealth was not limited, more of it could be created all the time ('wealth' could mean money, employment, education, healthcare for everyone, a cleaner world, a fairer world, and so on). They also believed firmly that more wealth would be created—*for everyone to share*—if people worked with each other rather than against each other. In other words, Adam Smith believed that wealth could be a 'win-win' game, or a *non* zero-sum game.

MERCANTILISM? THAT'S SO LAST CENTURY. FREE TRADE—NOW THAT'S THE TICKET!

Like Adam Smith, there had been other people who had been making snarky remarks about Mercantilism, but the reason we remember him and not them is that he was the first to actually come up with an alternative new way to do business. He called it 'Free Trade'.

Free Trade basically said that countries and people should trade with each other freely and plentifully. Both sides should sell to each other, and both sides should buy from each other, with no restrictions from governments. That was the only way for all countries, and all people, to get more productive, more efficient, and more wealthy.

'This is why Free Trade works, dummies!'* And other wise things Adam Smith said.

The Wealth of Nations was a fat book, and Smith said many, many things in it. Here are a few of the important ones. They seem like complete no-brainers now, but they were revolutionary when he first said them.

▸ Everyone—the butcher, the baker, the candlestick maker—works only because of what he can get out of it for himself. A baker, for instance, doesn't make bread because he wants to be nice to you and/or feed you, he does so because he wants to sell it to you and make money for himself.

▸ Staying with our baker, no baker supports ideas like 'Let's not allow bakers from other countries to sell their bread in our country, we make perfectly good bread here' out of a great pride in his country. He supports it because he doesn't want the competition! If a foreign baker can make bread better or sell it cheaper than our baker, and you allow him to come in, our baker is sunk, right?

▸ Here's the thing, though—competition is good! For everyone, but *especially* for the 'consumer'. A consumer is anyone who buys (consumes) products that different producers produce—products like food, movies, furniture, plane journeys, cows, iPhones, beach vacations, homes, whatever. The basic aim of a producer, we all know, is to attract a consumer.

---

*Okay, maybe he didn't use exactly those words.

When there is competition, producers will:

- Produce good products (because otherwise consumers will buy someone else's better products)
- Sell their products for as low a price as possible (because otherwise consumers will buy someone else's cheaper product, especially if both products are more or less the same quality)

Win-win for consumer! What about the poor producers? They do well too! How? Well, every producer is also a consumer (of his own products as well as other producers' products). So if *all* consumers benefit in a 'competitive market' (a marketplace for goods where every seller of things is putting the consumer first), these 'producer-consumers' do too!

▸ But if everyone works only for his own selfish reasons and not to make his country rich, how will the country prosper? Isn't it better that the government, which knows what is best for the country, tells people what to produce, how much of it to produce, when to produce it, and how much to charge for the finished product? No way! In fact, people work hardest, and most efficiently, producing just the right amount of goods, at just the right price, at just the right time, in the least stressful way possible, and so on, when they are working for what *they* want—more money, more time to watch football, more customers. And when every citizen is working hard and working efficiently, how can the country *not* prosper?

You see? You see why Mercantilism sucks and Free Trade rocks? Told ya!

LEARN THE LINGO

Laissez-faire*

In 1681, when Mercantilism (literally) ruled the waves, a group of French merchants led by a Monsieur Le Gendre were in a meeting with the powerful French finance minister Jean Baptiste-Colbert. Eagerly, Colbert asked the merchants how the French government could help them so that they could go out and make even more money from far-flung colonies. Le Gendre, who, like the other merchants, was getting a little tired of the government interfering in trade, is supposed to have sighed, and famously replied, '*Laissez-nous faire!*' (*Just allow us to do what we want to do! Please!*)

Yup, exactly what Adam Smith recommended to his government a century later, with his 'Free Trade' idea. *Stop interfering in business, you dunderheads!* This whole idea of governments 'letting go' of control and allowing people themselves to decide what to produce and what price to sell it at is called 'Laissez-faire Economics'.

MOVE OVER, ADAM SMITH, DAVID RICARDO IS IN THE HOUSE!

So Adam Smith was human, so he didn't get *everything* right *all* the time. One of the things he got wrong was the answer to this question: When we are talking countries, when is it a good idea for one country (let's call it Desh)

---

*The term 'laissez-faire' (say 'lay-say-fair') is also used in regular English, to mean 'laid-back' or 'allowing things to take their own course, without interfering too much' as in, 'a laissez-faire attitude to life'.

to trade with another (let's call it Videsh)?

Here's what Adam Smith said: Desh and Videsh should trade with each other if:

▶ Desh is 'better' at producing a good* than Videsh, i.e., when Desh can make a product in an easier, faster or cheaper way than Videsh.

▶ Videsh is better than Desh at producing a different good.

Situation 1

Let's say, for example, that Desh is 'better' at producing cotton cloth than Videsh, and Videsh is better at producing cheese than Desh (even though Desh also produces its own cheese and Videsh also produces its own cotton). If we drew up a table of comparison, it would look like this.

DESH'S COTTON FABRIC...	VIDESH'S CHEESE...
• Is cheaper	• Is cheaper
• Is produced faster	• Has a better flavour
• Is better	• Has more varieties
...than Videsh's cotton fabric.	...than Desh's cheese.

Adam Smith's logic works well in this example (see picture), but it gets a little iffy in this one: what if Desh is better at producing both cloth *and* cheese? Smith would say that Desh should make both and not trade with Videsh at all. In fact, he would argue that Desh *would* not trade with Videsh.

---

*No, there's nothing wrong with the grammar in that sentence. Neither have we suddenly switched over to moral science. 'Good' in this case is the singular form of 'goods', which is another word for products. So 'good' here simply means a product. We shall keep using 'good' in this way through the book.

In real life, however, that is not what happens.

Let's put countries aside for a minute, and think about our own individual lives. Let's talk about you and your sister (if you don't have one, use your imagination. In the study of Economics, as we will see, imagination is very important). Let's say the two of you want to surprise Mom on her birthday with a fresh-baked cake and a spic-and-span house. BUT. You have to get it all done in the one hour you have between your coming home from school and Mom getting home from work.

Situation 1

SISTER	Better at tidying
YOU	Better at baking

Solution: Sister tidies up, you bake. Mom gets home to a clean house and a fresh-baked cake. Hurray!

Situation 2

SISTER	Better at tidying AND baking
YOU	Bad at both

Most often, countries behave like your sister, too. Even if Desh is better at producing *both* cloth and cheese, Desh will sometimes decide to buy (more expensive, not so flavourful) cheese from Videsh! Why does this happen?

The chap who figured out the answer, some forty years after *The Wealth of Nations* was published, was a British economist called David Ricardo. He said this happens because of *choices* people and countries make, based on a concept called **opportunity cost**. The short definition of opportunity cost is: 'what you give up to get something else'. In a world full of scarcity, said Ricardo, where everyone has limited money, limited time, and limited energy, one has to *always* give up something to get something.* The good part is that you can usually choose what you want to give up.

---

*No, we still haven't wandered off into a moral science class.

The choice, dear Brutus, is not in our stars but in ourselves

Let's go back to Mum's birthday. If she had more time, or more energy, your sister may have followed Adam Smith's advice and done both. But there is only one hour before Mum gets home (scarcity of time), and your sister definitely does not want to slog on her own while you watch TV scarcity of energy, especially as the end result will then be either a wonderfully tidy house and a half-baked (haha!) cake, or a lovely cake and an untidy house. Neither of these results is appealing.

So to make the best use of the resources at hand (an hour of time, her skills, your skills, her energy, and your energy), you decide to split the work.

Situation 1

SISTER: You are not as good as I am at tidying up, but you are almost as good at baking, so you bake while I tidy up.
Result 1: Almost perfect cake, perfectly clean house
Opportunity Cost (or what you both decide to give up, for the result you both want): Perfect cake

Situation 2

SISTER: You are not as good as I am at baking, but you are almost as good at tidying up, so you tidy up while I bake.
Result 1: Passably tidy house, perfect cake
Opportunity Cost (or what you both decide to give up, for the result you both want): Perfectly tidy house

Overall result in either case: Win-win.

Mum's thrilled (she doesn't care whether the cake is perfect or not, or whether the house is perfectly tidy or not, she's just going 'awww' that you made the effort), and you and sis are happy—you both worked hard and gave Mum the best birthday surprise you could have given her, despite the constraints. The best possible outcome for both sides!

The same logic works with countries, too. Desh may be better at producing both cotton and cheese, but maybe there is more money to be made selling cheese to other countries rather than cloth. Maybe Desh can become way richer by selling lots and lots of cheese across the world than by selling some cheese and some cloth. In such a case, Desh would rather put all its people to work making cheese, and buy cotton from Videsh, even though Videsh's cotton costs more than its own. In other words, for Desh, the opportunity cost of making cotton (all the lovely moolah it is possible to make by making more cheese) is way higher than the opportunity cost of buying Videsh's cotton (a slightly bigger spend on cotton). And for Videsh, even though it isn't the cheapest cotton cloth-producing country in the world, this means a lucrative trade in cotton with Desh. Everyone wins!

More Opportunity Cost (OC) questions to think about

Why do people who can drive their own cars perfectly well hire a driver? Obviously because the OC of driving themselves is huge. In their minds, it is bigger than the OC of spending money on a good driver. (*Just as an exercise to help you understand the OC concept better, list five 'opportunities' that someone gives up when they drive their own car. To start you off, here are two: the opportunity to take a nap while getting from one place to another, the opportunity to pass on the responsibility of finding a parking spot to someone else.)*

In a similar vein:

▸ Why do mums (or dads) who cook perfectly well choose to order takeout on weekends?

▸ Why do doctor/engineer/scientist parents, who can surely coach their own children in math and science, choose to send them out for tuitions in these subjects instead?

▸ Why do you choose to wake up early to do homework when you could have done it just as easily the previous night?

If you think about it, the answers to these apparently 'non-Economics' questions are selfish ones, all of them based on an Economics concept called Opportunity Cost! You can't escape from Economics!

AND FINALLY—DRUMROLL PLEASE—THE REAL POINT OF THIS SECTION

This is the bottomline—everyone wants to 'win'. Everyone—farmers, schools, factories, cricket teams, countries—wants to use the resources that they have at their disposal—money, time, talent, skills, brains, energy, machines, land—in the best possible way to get the result they want. Because resources are limited and wants are unlimited (economists call this 'the problem of scarcity'), everyone is forced to allocate the resources wisely and to make tough choices, i.e., give up certain things to get other things *that they want more*. Which is what David Ricardo was talking about.

Who is this 'everyone' who is making these choices? Economists divide 'everyone' into three main 'agents':

Households (individual people, families): should we go on a holiday to Kashmir (the opportunity to see a new part of India, but the fun ends in a week) or buy a 40-inch TV (24/7 entertainment but without the joy of actual travel) this year?

Firms (companies, factories, etc): should we manufacture all our products ourselves (makes us a bigger profit) or buy some of them from another company and put our name on the package (saves us time, effort, and money to buy machinery)?

Countries (governments): to generate electricity, should we build big dams (which involve flooding of forests and villages but uses a renewable resource, water) or nuclear plants (which use a non-renewable resource and generate toxic waste, but produce more energy from less fuel)?

THE CHOICE MAKERS

All three are essentially making one key choice: a choice between what economists call 'jam today' and 'jam tomorrow'.

Eh? Economics is about jam?

Well, yes, in a manner of speaking. Here's how it works. Let's talk about individuals, or households, first. As a household, you have to make a choice between blowing up a lot of money on something that you don't really need but will bring you a lot of happiness right now (jam today) and buying something cheaper and putting the extra money aside for things you might need in the future (jam tomorrow).

Firms have to make such choices too. For instance, let's say Biscuit Factory A, which has been the market leader so far, is facing competition from Biscuit Factory B, which is producing more biscuits than A is and filling up supermarket shelves with them. Now Factory A will have to decide whether to start spending its money on extra flour, butter and sugar, and work its existing machines to the maximum (and possibly cause them to break down quicker), so that they can quickly make a ton more biscuits to compete with Factory B (i.e., jam today) or to spend money on buying more and better machines that will, over the next year, help them to produce not only more biscuits than B but many different types of biscuits, which will help them beat the competition in the long run (i.e., jam tomorrow).

Policy-makers in different countries have to make similar choices. For example:

▸ Should they encourage the spending of money on setting up factories that will make lots of money, but will also almost certainly end up polluting the land, water and air (in other words, 'jam today', since the environmental problems won't come back to bother you for a few years yet); OR

▸ Should they recommend that money be spent on developing 'clean technology', which will ensure that any factory that comes up in the future will pollute as little as possible, thus making for a better planet for everyone in ten years' time (jam tomorrow).

Obviously, the right choice in all these cases lies in choosing smartly and wisely—using both head and heart—so that there is a little bit of jam today but also a little bit left over for tomorrow, not just for the person who makes that choice, but for everyone else too. The study of how households, firms, governments and all the others in between choose to spread their jam, why they spread it the way they do, and how those choices can tell us how they will spread their jam in the future... (aaaarghhhhh! enough with the jam already!) is what Economics is all about.

Sounds like Economics is about a lot more than just money being exchanged for goods, doesn't it? In fact, it feels like it has bits of psychology in it, even philosophy! Maybe you are even beginning to believe that the passionate economist in the introduction to this book wasn't entirely joking. Well, let's see in the next couple of sections, shall we?

Bet you didn't know that!
How Economics gave Darwin his Big Idea

In ye olde England in the eighteenth century lived a priest called Thomas Malthus. Reverend Malthus was a scholar in different fields, including Economics, and much respected by the community. In 1798, after he published an essay called *The Principle of Population*, he suddenly found himself quite famous. The essay itself was quite a gloom-and-doom one—after a ton of mathematical analysis and deduction, Malthus had concluded that human population was growing way too quickly for the world to produce enough food for everyone. Therefore, said Malthus, humans were condemned to a life of great hunger and misery unless population was controlled.

This statement was taken literally by rich, mean landlords, who made life miserable for their poor labourers, reasoning that if the poor fell ill and died as a result of the oppression, it was a good thing, since that was one way of controlling the population and making sure there was enough food for the others. After all, argued the landlords, the poor, with their lack of education, hygiene and terrible sense of fashion, didn't deserve to live even half as much as the sophisticated, intelligent rich did. Charming men, these landlords, don't you think?

Funnily enough, when Charles Darwin read the same essay, it sparked off an entirely different train of thought in his head. He saw instantly that the same constraints—uncontrolled population increase and a limited supply of food—applied in the animal and plant kingdoms. Unlike in the human world, however, animals and plants could not decide to have fewer children and thus conserve their resources. Neither could they learn to grow more food using science and technology. But somehow, Nature still managed to maintain that perfect balance of food and animals.

That realization gave Darwin his 'Eureka!' moment. The way things worked out in Nature, he figured, was through a system that he called 'natural selection'. Species of animals and plants that could not deal with the competition for limited food and resources from other species completely died out. But those that adapted, i.e., cleverly got rid of those features that hindered their survival, and kept or added features that helped them win the competition for resources, became the 'fittest' species, and were 'selected' by Nature to survive into the future. And that was how population was controlled in the natural world! This idea became the basis of his theory of evolution and his big fat book *The Origin of Species**.

You see? Economics strikes again!

---

*This book also has a much longer name, but we can make do nicely with this short, sweet version.

WHAT COUNTRIES THINK ABOUT WHEN THEY THINK ABOUT ECONOMICS (A.K.A. MACROECONOMICS)

There are many ways to split the bulky 'Study of Economics' pie to make it easier for wide-eyed newbies to consume and digest. One popular way is to divide it into Macroeconomics and Microeconomics.

What is Macroeconomics? It is a macro (the Greek word for 'large') way of looking at how Economics works. Macroeconomics is not concerned with what individuals or households spend each month on soap or how many packets of biscuits a factory makes in a year. It is concerned with larger and way more complex issues, like how the price of a barrel of oil in Saudi Arabia affects the price of onions in India, how the fear of terrorism in France affects airline companies in the USA, how India becoming the first country in Asia to send a mission to Mars affects its trade relations with China, and so on.

Such issues are way too complex for this book to handle, but what we will try and do is find the not-always-simple answers to four simple questions that skim the surface of Macroeconomics. Here goes.

BIG QUESTION 1

Where does the government get its money from? And what does it do with it once it has it?

Hmmm. That's something to think about, isn't it? After all, the government is in a sort of special position—it can't go to work like normal people and earn a salary every month. Sure, a government could own farms where it grows things (rice, apples, sugarcane) or factories where it manufactures stuff (toothpaste, paper, cars) and earn money for itself by selling them in the market. The governments of many countries do earn money this way, but there's something inherently unfair about that. Since it is the government that makes the rules on how to do business in a country, what's to prevent it from making rules that would help its own companies? It would be like having the referee in a football match playing as part of one of the teams.

That is why several governments don't own too many factories or farms, preferring to let the people of their countries compete among themselves, thus keeping it all fair. How do these governments earn money, then? We shall come to that, but in the meanwhile, let us consider the second part of the question: what does a government spend its money on?

First of all, on salaries. The government has hundreds of thousands of employees—politicians, bureaucrats, policemen, firemen, soldiers, station masters (at railway stations), sweepers (who clean your streets), doctors (who work in government hospitals), teachers (who work in government schools), scientists (who work in space research and development, for instance), and they all need to be paid salaries.

Secondly, governments need money to spend on building 'infrastructure'—new roads, parks, bridges and dams (because who else will build them?), providing streetlights, laying pipes to transport clean water from rivers and reservoirs to our homes and other pipes to take used water and sewage away. They need money to buy x-ray machines for government hospitals and benches for government schools, apart from fighter planes, aircraft carriers, submarines, jeeps and tanks for the armed forces. They need money to invest in space exploration and scientific research, which will bring great benefits for the country in the future. They need emergency money stored up which can be used in the event of natural calamities like floods or earthquakes. Phew!

So, we have established that governments need money. Now let's go back to the question of where the government gets its money from. Quite obviously, it gets it from the people who are enjoying the services it provides—us! There is no such thing as a free lunch in this world, and we have to pay for the pleasure of having a neighbourhood park and the security of having brave soldiers defending our borders while we sleep. The government has found a simple, straightforward way of getting us to pay for all this—taxes!

You have to pay a tax if:

▶ You earn a salary or have any other income except agricultural income (income tax)

▶ You manufacture anything in India (excise duty)
▶ You sell anything in India (sales tax / value added tax, VAT)
▶ You bring anything into India from outside (customs duty)
▶ You transport what you manufacture from one state to another (octroi)
▶ You own a car, or a house, or non-agricultural land (property tax)
▶ You use the road (road tax)
▶ You go to watch a movie (entertainment tax)
▶ You eat out at a restaurant in a fancy hotel (luxury tax)
▶ The government decides to raise money for a specific project, like Swachh Bharat (Swachh Bharat cess)

And so on.

Governments also get money into their kitty by:

▶ Selling off companies they own
▶ Borrowing from the people of the country by selling them 'government bonds'*

---

*Government bonds are bits of paper, each worth a certain amount of money. When people have some cash to spare, they buy these bonds, thus 'lending' the government their money. Why? Because the government guarantees that when you bring the bonds back to them, they will return the amount of money you spent on buying them, plus a little extra. But there are conditions: the 'little extra' is a fixed amount, and you can't ask for your money back until a certain time has passed. Basically, it's a good way to save your spare cash, i.e., to lock some money away for the future. Of course, you can also just put your money under your mattress and take it out in the future, but if you buy government bonds, or put it in a bank, your money will also grow, not just sit there getting mouldy. Bonds are popular because their value is guaranteed by the government, which means your money is as safe as it can be.

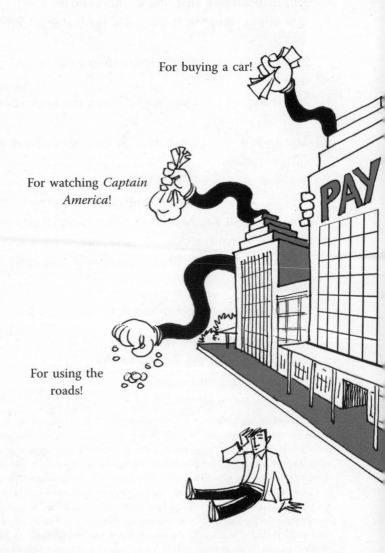

For eating out at a
five-star hotel!

For bringing iPhone 7
into the country!

For wanting a clean
country!

▶ Borrowing from other countries or 'financial institutions' like the World Bank or the International Monetary Fund

▶ Charging a fee to anyone who wants to mine metal ores or extract petroleum or natural gas

▶ Charging 'spectrum fees' (see page 51)

A good question to ask now would be: how much money does the Indian government actually raise using all these different methods? Maybe you should sit down before you read the number—it is so large it might cause your head to spin. In 2015, it totalled up to—drumroll please—28.1 trillion rupees (a trillion is 1 followed by 12 zeros) or 410 billion US Dollars (USD)! But here's what's even more interesting—the government's expenses in the same period were way higher at 38.3 trillion rupees (USD 560 billion)! Apparently, countries are just as good at living beyond their means as we are.*

---

*The gap between the money a country earns and the money it spends, which economists call 'fiscal deficit', is not unique to India. In fact, most countries have an annual fiscal deficit, i.e., each year, they spend more than they earn. That's not necessarily a bad thing, though. You see, deficits often arise because a government has invested a lot of money in 'jam tomorrow', i.e. projects like education, healthcare, scientific research, space exploration etc, which will begin to earn money for the country only in the distant future. In fact, economists argue that such a deficit is required for an economy to grow. It is only when the deficit happens without investment in the future that it becomes something to worry about.

LEARN THE LINGO

Spectrum Auctions

An interesting, and fairly new, way for governments to raise money is by conducting 'spectrum auctions'. The spectrum we're talking about here is the electromagnetic spectrum—the medium through which wireless signals are transmitted through the air. Every time you listen to music on your car radio, watch digital TV, make a call on your mobile phone, or use Google Maps to get directions on the highway, you are using the electromagnetic spectrum. Unfortunately, there is only a limited number of signals that can go back and forth on the available spectrum. If there are too many signals, the spectrum gets jammed and your YouTube video will keep buffering instead of playing.

Telecommunication companies like Airtel, Bharti, BSNL, and so on, all want to control as much of the spectrum as possible so that their customers have the best experience. So they go and bid big money to 'buy' chunks of the spectrum at 'spectrum auctions' that the government organizes. Whoever offers to pay the highest amount of money for a chunk is the one the government sells the chunk to. Once a company has 'bought' a chunk, no one else is allowed to transmit on it except that company. Yup, 'ruling the airwaves' just got a whole new meaning.

Bet you didn't know that!

Only 3 per cent of Indians pay income tax!

If you earn an income in India, you are supposed to pay part of it to the government as income tax. The only people who don't have to pay are those who earn their income through agriculture. Yes, India doesn't tax farmers, whether they are poor peasants labouring in the landlord's fields, or the wealthy landlord who owns hundreds of acres of farmland and makes tons of money every month. This is a decision the founding fathers of our country took when India first became free—since most of the country then was poor and depended on agriculture for a living, they didn't want to burden them any more than necessary.

Even today, almost 70 per cent of Indians depend on agriculture for their livelihood. That means 70 per cent automatically pays no income tax. Of the 30 per cent who don't depend on agriculture, only about 3 per cent pay their income tax. Everyone else either (1) earns too little to pay the tax (only people who earn above a certain amount of money per year are taxed), (2) is *pretending* that he earns too little to pay the tax (cheater!), or (3) is counting on the fact that the government is too busy to catch him and force him to pay (avoider).

The government is constantly trying to figure out how to 'get more people into the tax net', so that they can have more money to spend on things the country desperately needs. But because it is so difficult, the government compensates by taxing us 'indirectly' (via taxes like sales tax, luxury tax, VAT and service tax). Look at your bill when you eat out at a restaurant next time and calculate what percentage of your bill is just the tax part.

If your parents pay income tax (ask them!), they are part of a very small percentage of Indians who are doing the right thing—be proud!

LEARN THE LINGO

Black Money

Sounds quite sinister, that. But it is also a phrase we hear a *lot* in India, in casual conversation, especially since the demonetisation of November 2016. And small wonder, because according to reports, India has more black money than the rest of the world *combined*!

Yayy! Another thing that India is World No. 1 at!

Erm, actually, it's nothing to rejoice about. To see why, you have to first know what black money really means.

In general, black money essentially means all the money that has been earned on the black market. The 'black market'

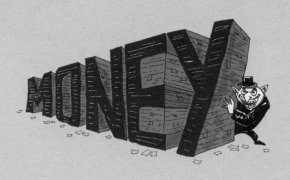

is the umbrella name for a 'marketplace' where trade in all kinds of illegal things—guns, drugs, women, children, human organs like kidneys, animal parts like elephant tusks and rhino horn, alcohol, tobacco, petrol, counterfeit medicine, currency, fake passports—happens, without governments knowing. Anyone who indulges in these activities whether as buyers, sellers or transporters, is considered a member of the 'illegal economy'.

Another illegal way to make tons of black money, (or money that the government doesn't know about) which is very popular in our country, is through corruption. Many government officials, who are already paid a salary by the government, make more money on the side by asking you to pay them an extra something 'under the table' in cash. In return for such a bribe, they will make sure that your work gets done smoothly (for instance, you will get your driver's licence without even showing up at the RTO) or that your firm gets picked over several others to supply a huge order of steel or cement for a government project like building a road or a flyover.

There is another kind of black money, too. This is money that someone has earned in a legal way, but hasn't told the government about, so that she doesn't have to pay income tax on it.

If your parents work for a company that pays them their salary by cheque at the end of each month, or deposits money directly in their bank accounts, they can't hide what they earn from the government. But if they work for themselves, and receive money for whatever goods and services they are selling in cash, or if they work for someone who pays them in cash, there is no way for the government to know exactly how much they are earning—the government will simply have to believe what your parents tell them.

By law, this way of avoiding income tax by not 'declaring' your entire income to the government, even if you have earned the money in a perfectly legal way, makes you as much of a criminal as someone who smuggles drugs into the country. And yet so many Indians continue to do it!

It was all these kinds of black money that the government was trying to curb and destroy through its 'demonetisation' move (see page 56 for more details) in November 2016.

Now, what do you think these criminals do with all their black money?

▶ They spend it, live life king-size! (Nope, that would only get the tax officers all suspicious.)
▶ They stuff it into their mattresses! (Yes—that's what many of them actually do!)
▶ They put it into a bank! (Erm, no, because then the government will know they have it. Duh!)

Actually, most 'black money criminals' either:

▶ 'Launder their money', turning it from 'black' to 'white', i.e., figure out a way to make it seem that they got this illegal money in a legal way, and then spend it on whatever they want to; or
▶ Put their illegal money into Swiss banks. (Swiss bank accounts only have numbers to them, and no names,

to protect the identity of their clients. It is a criminal offence in Switzerland for a bank to reveal the name of the account holder.)

According to reports, Indians have more money in Swiss banks than citizens of any other country in the world. One estimate puts it at 130 billion rupees! By taking this money out of the country, these Indians have made 130 billion rupees (or whatever the exact amount is) worth of funds unavailable to the Indian government or to Indian industry. If it was available, India could arguably pay off most of its national debt and become one of the world's richest and most developed countries. And we haven't even begun to talk about all the black money that is inside Indian mattresses, and in Indian money-laundering 'washing machines'!

You see? You think a grown-up slipping a policeman a hundred bucks to ensure that he doesn't give a ticket (for talking on the phone while driving, say) is a small thing which doesn't matter to anyone, but what he is actually doing is donating to the country's illegal economy by helping the policeman earn black money. Like so many other things in life, the illegal economy also begins with us, and the choices we make. Think about it.

A short note on Demonetisation

On the evening of 8 November 2016, in a shock announcement that sent ripples of fear and excitement through the country, Prime Minister Narendra Modi let Indians know that, from that very midnight onwards, currency notes of the value ₹500 and ₹1000 would be 'demonetised'—they could not be used anymore as a medium of exchange for goods and services. If you had any of those notes with you, you could, however, exchange them for new currency notes of the same value in banks and post offices, or deposit them into your bank account, where they would be counted according to their printed value. This, he said, was part of the country's war against black money.

Economists, bankers, politicians and common people had differing views on the timing of the demonetisation, and the way in which it was carried out. But these views needn't concern us now.

Instead, let's think about how demonetisation helps to bring out the black money in the system and how that helps the country.

▸ When black money is stored as cash, it is stored as high-value notes; i.e., as ₹500 notes or as ₹1000 notes. That way, money takes up far less space. (If it was stored as ₹10 notes, the mattress inside which they were hidden would become very thick indeed.)

▸ When such high-value notes are demonetised, all of them instantly become worthless pieces of paper. The only way they will regain their value is when they are deposited in banks (or exchanged at banks for new currency of equivalent value).

▸ If you deposited the devalued notes into your account, the government would know that that money was part of your income, and you would then have to pay tax on it. If you did not deposit them into your account, they would remain completely worthless. Generally, more people would prefer to deposit their black money and pay a part of it as tax, thus getting some value for it, rather than not deposit it and get no value for it at all.

▸ If plenty of previously undeclared money made its way into the banks and swelled the bank's coffers, banks would have more money to lend to people who wanted to start new businesses or schools or hospitals, or build houses, or buy farmland. (If you're not quite sure what banks do and how they work, check out page 137.) All that activity in education, healthcare, manufacturing, building, and farming would help the country produce more goods and services both for the use of people in the country and for export to other countries. That would help the economy grow.

▸ Banks would also have to pay more tax to the government (how much tax a bank pays depends on how much money it has). Therefore, the government also would have more money to spend on projects that the country needs.

▸ A lot of the undeclared money may *not* come back to the banks, either, because people who have it will not want the government to know that they had it in the first place. Let's say this money which does not come back amounts to ₹X crores. That means the banks (or at least the Reserve Bank of India) is making a saving, or a 'profit', of ₹X crores, since it doesn't have to pay out that amount of money to the people who had it.

There are also other possible side benefits of demonetisation.

▸ Any counterfeit ₹500 and ₹1000 notes in circulation would become completely valueless overnight. Counterfeiters would have to wait for the government to release new notes and figure out how to duplicate them before they started printing counterfeits again, and this would take time. Within that time, the government could bring in stricter rules to crack down on counterfeiting.

▸ Millions of people in India do not have bank accounts. Since the only way of getting value for devalued ₹500 and ₹1000 notes is to deposit it in a bank account, demonetisation could encourage people to open accounts and deposit their money in them. This would help banks to earn money, which they can then lend out to people who need them. It would also help the government to monitor the amount of money in the system.

▸ Keeping money in banks and withdrawing only the amount you need when you need it—or paying for something by simply transferring money from your account to the payee's account—is safer and more secure than carrying actual cash around.

▸ Having a bank account and showing that you are serious about putting away a little money in it regularly will help you get a loan from a bank when you need it. A bank loan is far safer, and less expensive than a loan from a random moneylender.

▸ More people would begin to spend digital money instead of cash, through debit cards, credit cards, or online wallets. This would again help the government monitor how much money is being earned and spent, and by whom, which it would not have been able to do if cash had been exchanged. Knowing how much each person earns will also help the government catch tax avoiders and make them pay. Digital money will also thwart counterfeiters—there is no place for fake currency in a 'cashless society'.

On the flip side, there are many problems, too, with demonetisation, especially in the weeks immediately following such a drastic move. This is what was happening when this book went into print.

▶ Since ₹500 and ₹1000 notes made up, in value, more than 80 per cent of the total cash circulating in India, removing them overnight created a severe shock to the economy. People had no cash to buy things, and didn't know when they would be able to get more, so they reduced spending.

▶ There were long lines in banks of those who wanted to either deposit old notes into their accounts, exchange old notes for new ones, or withdraw money from their accounts. Banks did not have big reserves of new currency, so there was a limit on how much each person could withdraw. ATMs ran out of money very quickly. Many of them were not refilled for days.

▶ The new ₹2000 note, which was introduced soon after the demonetisation announcement, helped matters along, but the new ₹500 note, which was meant to replace the old ₹500 note, took a long time coming. For many weeks, therefore, finding change (for ₹2000) was a real issue.

▸ Since a huge percentage of India still trades only in cash, the scarcity of cash was a problem, and caused the economy to slow down in the first few weeks. Everyone's business was affected—from the small trader to the big builder, from the farmer to the factory owner. It prompted a lot of people to switch to digital buying and selling and to go cashless, but many more millions need to get there. They will not find it easy to do that for the following reason.

• For a country to go 'cashless', a majority of its households should have at least one bank account each; a majority of its people should have smartphones through which they can send and receive 'digital' money instead of cash (or there should be a platform that will work on regular phones); and there should be strong Internet connectivity everywhere, because all these transactions are done over the Internet. India does quite well on the first two counts, but Internet connectivity is still poor in large areas of the country, which means it will still be a while before it is able to go truly cashless. Even if we had had great Internet connectivity (or a platform that used just the cellphone network) already up and running, it would still take a ton of time to ensure that all banks were hooked up to it and that all users knew how exactly to work it.

All these short-term problems were expected, however. Economists say that we cannot truly analyse how good or bad demonetisation was for the country—did it bring hidden reserves of black money into the open (and how much)? Did it go some way in curbing corruption? Did it succeed in curbing the production of counterfeit currency? How did it affect the economy?—until at least six months after the fact, i.e., in May or June 2017.

So was demonetisation a good move? You tell us in July 2017!

Bet you didn't know that!

MRP: It happens only in India

Have you noticed that any packaged good that you buy—soft drinks, biscuits, shampoo, medicines—has a price printed or stuck on it, which is preceded by the initials MRP? Ever wondered what it meant? Well, even if you never wondered, here's the answer: MRP stands for Maximum Retail Price, and it means what it says. To 'retail' means to 'sell', so the MRP is the maximum price at which a good can be sold.

Who decides what that price is? If it was the government that decided the price, that would make India a 'government-controlled command economy' (see 'Economic Systems' on page 70), which we aren't. If it was the retailer, or the seller of the product, who decided the price, that would make it a 'market economy', which India is heading towards strongly but hasn't entirely become yet. In India, (which, by the way, is the *only* country in the world that has an MRP system) the MRP is actually decided by the manufacturer of the product. Here's how they do it.

If ₹X = What the manufacturer wants to charge for the product, and

₹Y = An extra amount that the retailer gets to keep for himself every time he sells the product, as a fee for all the work he does to buy, transport, store and sell the product to you, then

MRP = ₹X + ₹Y

The Indian government introduced the MRP system in 1990, for very good reasons (explained below). But a lot of people think that the MRP should be done away with, for several other good reasons (explained below too). Let's check out both sides of the argument, shall we?

All those in favour say 'Aye'!

The MRP was introduced, essentially, to protect the customer. Let's say you lived in a remote village where there were only one or two shops selling essentials. Without access to good roads and technology, you would not know what those essentials cost in the nearest town. Without a printed MRP to keep him honest, the shopkeeper in your village would sell you those items at whatever price he wanted! The Indian government introduced the MRP system in 1990 to prevent stuff like that from happening. There's another reason. A fixed MRP prevents one powerful retailer from bulldozing every other retailer out of existence, thus keeping things fair for retailers as well. How does that work?

Let's say there are two shopkeepers in your remote village, but one (let's call him Ameer) is far wealthier than the other (let's call him Less Ameer). Now, any shopkeeper (or retailer) would calculate the price of his products using this equation.

$$CP + RC + P = RP$$

where:

- CP is Cost Price (or what it cost him to buy the product from the manufacturer)
- RC is Retailer Cost (or what it cost him to buy, transport, store and sell the product at your village)
- P is Profit, and
- RP is the final Retail Price

This is the equation that Less Ameer (LA) would use too. However, our wealthy Ameer may tweak the equation a little. Since Ameer has 'deep pockets', i.e., more money than LA, he may decide not to add his Profit to the equation. He does not want to lose money (which is why he keeps CP and RC), but he may not mind about not *making* money for a while. Naturally, things will be cheaper (RP will be less) in Ameer's shop, and all customers will flock there. After a few months of swatting flies, LA will be forced to shut down his shop and go become an assistant to a halwai (since he has so much experience swatting flies). Or something. At this point, our greedy bully Ameer will add the P to his equation, and sell his products at the same price as LA had sold them.

So far so good. All this can—and does—happen whether

or not there is an MRP. Here's where it begins to get interesting, though, and the MRP really begins to show its strength. Now, because he is the only shop around, Ameer can push the P up to whatever level he likes, and villagers like you will have no choice but to buy from him! This cannot happen when there is an MRP.

A fixed MRP, therefore, keeps the playing field fair and prevents this kind of bullying and profiteering by powerful retailers. And that's why the MRP should stay!

All those not in favour say 'Nay'!

And this is how the naysayers argue their point.

- The MRP works only on packaged items. In India, many other essentials—vegetables and fruits, for instance—are sold loose, and retailers charge what they like anyway, depending on how much they paid for it and how much the customer is willing to pay. Also, even in cities, except in the big supermarkets, things like dals, pulses, rice, oil and spices are sold loose, not in packets with an MRP marked. This sort of defeats the purpose of the MRP.

- These days, with mobile phones and television and radio reaching even small villages, most people know what prices of things ought to be. It is far more unlikely that retailers can cheat their customers now.

- It is really difficult for the government to ensure that everyone is sticking to the MRP, especially in smaller towns and villages. Instead of spending money, time, and effort to enforce the MRP, the government can invest in technology to ensure that information on the right price of a good reaches customers in far-flung villages.

- India is moving towards becoming a free market, where the 'market' (people who buy and sell goods) decides what the price of something should be. In other words, if people are willing to pay more for something, its price should go up, and if people will not (or cannot) buy something because its price is too high, its price should go down.

- Who knows how much people are willing to pay for something? Is it the manufacturer, who is not in touch with the customer directly, or the retailer, who meets customers every day? Obviously, it is the latter. Doesn't it make sense, then, for the retailer to have the freedom to decide the price, not the manufacturer? A fixed MRP—or a pre-decided price—is an 'artificial' price, say the naysayers. It simply won't work as well, they argue, as the 'natural' price set by the retailer, which is a flexible price that can go up or down depending on the mood of the customer. And that's why the MRP should go!

Now that you have heard both sides of the MRP argument, what are your thoughts? Should the MRP stay, or go?

BIG QUESTION 2

How come my parents never ate a Maharaja Mac in India when they were my age?

Because they were vegetarian, haha.

No, but seriously, it was because foreign companies were

simply not allowed to trade in India until quite recently!

It might be a little difficult for you to imagine, but many of your parents spent their entire childhoods (in India) never having eaten a burger (not even a veggie one) from McDonalds, or dug into a bucket of fried chicken from KFC, or even, hold your breath, guzzled a bottle of Pepsi or Coca Cola. How come, and what did Economics have to do with it? To understand it somewhat, we need to go back a bit in time.

Rewind to the mid-sixteenth century. Although Europeans were trading actively with India by that time, it was not until the end of the eighteenth century, 250 years later, that the British emerged as the most powerful European power in the subcontinent. By this time, they had also morphed from being mere trading partners into absolute rulers. Slowly but surely, they began to make some pretty big changes to the Indian economy. And these were changes that would benefit them, not us.

No wonder then, that from being one of the world's largest economies in 1700, India had become one of the poorest, and relatively a much smaller economy, by the time the British left in 1947. Clearly, things needed to be improved, and fast.

Our first Prime Minister, Jawaharlal Nehru, dearly wanted India to become industrialised quickly, so that we could stop importing finished goods from other countries and start manufacturing them ourselves. Another important point on his agenda was that India should also produce all the food her people needed, by herself. He felt that at least in the beginning, the government should decide how most of India's money should be spent.

If the government didn't take control, felt Nehru, there was a big chance that the rich would grab everything, and India would go back to being a collection of small kingdoms, with the rich behaving like kings and stomping upon the poor. There was another, equally undesirable, possibility. Even those who had the money to produce goods like iron and steel, big machinery, or aeroplanes, and provide services like education, banking and railways that would help the country's growth, may not want to produce those particular goods because doing so would not immediately bring them a big profit. If the government took charge, however, it could put its money where the country needed it most—set up colleges and steel plants in smaller towns, helping those towns to grow, build airports in remote areas so that they were connected to the rest of the country, and in short, do the kinds of things that someone looking for a quick profit would never do in a million years. Yup, Adam Smith may not have approved of Nehru's Economics, but government help and support was exactly what the destroyed Indian economy needed at that time.

Since Indian industry was so underdeveloped, the government felt that, at least for a while, it should be allowed to find its feet and gain confidence without worrying about competition from foreign industries, which were more established, more aggressive, and far wealthier.* India had

---

*Remember what happened in the village with the two shopkeepers Ameer and Less Ameer? The same thing could have happened to us if we had let the foreign Ameers in right at the beginning.

just come out of a dark period where exactly that kind of competition had destroyed our industries, so this seemed like a great idea at the time.

And that's why your parents grew up eating Indian burgers and Dabur Chyawanprash, keeping all their valuables in a Godrej almirah, piling into Ambassador cars to go on family holidays, watching a single television channel called Doordarshan, and drinking fizzy drinks called Thums Up and Limca!

But don't believe your parents when they tell you what sad, deprived childhoods they had—that's just regular parental drama, so that they can tell you what an ungrateful child you are. In reality, they loved their Parle biscuits and their Thums Up, which explains why those brands are still around today!

Of course, after about fifty years of protecting our home-grown industries, India began to realize that lack of competition was not such a great idea any more. Without competition, our industries had become smug and complacent. They were happy making inferior products (why bother making our products better when they are already the best available here?), treating customers badly (they have no choice but to come back to us, anyway), and not trying at all to make a profit (the government will keep giving us money and not let us collapse, so why hassle ourselves?). What made it worse was that even smart *Indian* businessmen with good ideas and India's welfare in mind were restricted in many ways so that they would not be able to compete with the inefficient government-run industries.

So, in 1991, India finally decided to **liberalise**, or open up the economy, and let foreign companies come in and set up shop. Mollycoddled Indian industries would have to up their game and compete—or die trying. As expected, many inefficient industries died, but several others got their act together, and are still around, competing fiercely with the foreign ones and even expanding beyond Indian shores. With the new freedom to start companies without too much government interference, thousands of new, exciting Indian companies with fresh ideas on what the Indian customer would like also opened their doors.

In 2016, we celebrated a quarter century of liberalisation. Everyone agrees it has been a huge success and that it has made life far more comfortable, interesting and fun for all of us. After all, that's the reason you are getting to watch *Modern Family* and *Quantico* while snacking on Lay's chips and guzzling Pepsi!

LEARN THE LINGO

Economic Systems

When your parents were growing up, India had what was called a 'Protectionist Economy', where we protected our industries against competition from foreign ones. When we opened our doors to the world in 1991, we liberalised our economy, making it more the kind of economy our old friend Adam Smith would have liked. Basically, though, there are four main kinds of 'economic systems', or 'ways in which a country does business'. Here's a quick primer.

Traditional economy: Money? Wozzat?

Imagine a country where money doesn't exist. With no money to buy or sell things, the people of this country use the **barter** system, where Good A (coconuts, cooking oil, vegetables, steel vessels, and so on) is exchanged for Good B (mud pots, dining tables, books, iPads, and so on). It sounds cool and all, but how in heaven's name does one decide how many coconuts add up to the value of an iPad? Also, what if the iPad seller was not interested in coconuts, even if you offered him 10,000 of them in exchange for one iPad? Economists call this the **double coincidence of wants** problem. Unless Trader 1 wants coconuts *and* Trader 2 wants an iPad (i.e., unless there is a 'double coincidence of wants'), there can be no trade, and this economy will collapse, which is what has happened in most of the world. The traditional economy does not exist anymore except in small, primitive and self-sufficient rural communities which do not trade with the outside world.

In certain unusual circumstances, however, barter has resurfaced even in developed economies. During the severe financial crisis that hit Germany after World War II, the bankrupt country carried on trade with other countries through barter! During the financial crisis in Zimbabwe more recently (see box, page 97), newspapers actually carried advertisements that offered, for instance, a barrel of fuel in exchange for a ton of soya beans. When money loses its value, and for a limited time period, barter still works!

Command economy: My wish is your command

Imagine a country where the government, and not individual people, owns all the **means of production**—factories, machines, minerals, metals, crops, electricity, water, anything, basically, that is needed to produce something else. Imagine also that this government sits down periodically and decides what crops should be grown in the country, and how much, what minerals should be mined, and how much, what goods should be produced, and how much, and what each of these goods should be priced at. This grand plan is based on what the government thinks people need, and what they think will help the government earn the maximum amount of money through exports to other countries. Once the plan is ready, it is shared with the people, after which the people go off and grow, mine, make and sell the stuff that the government has ordered them to do.

This government also decides a salary for everyone—carpenters, house help, software engineers, doctors. If you are a house help, you get exactly the same salary as every other house help, whether you are a good help or a bad one, a hard-working help or a lazy one.

The logic is that the government has all the data about everything and everyone in the country, so naturally it is in the best position to make such a plan. Also, since the government is made up of carefully selected (not elected) smart people and has only its citizens' welfare in mind, this kind of planning will ensure that everyone in the country has a job, and a decent salary. There will be no rich and poor in such a society, no upper class and lower class. The country's wealth will be 'owned' equally by all its citizens, instead of by a few rich, greedy people who will oppress everyone else.

The theory sounds good on paper, and command economy is still practised in a few countries like China, Cuba and North Korea, all of which have a Communist* system of government.

In reality, no government really has all the data about anything, so they end up making several bad decisions. Even if a government does have all the data, trying to guess what people need is a hugely complicated exercise and likely to be completely off the mark. Maybe the government decides to make too little bread one month because their data tells them that rice has become more popular (so that lots of people who love bread are forced to go without). Or they may decide to make as many cars as they have always done

---

*Communism believes in a fair and equal society for everyone. In theory, it is very democratic—it is about everyone being equal and everyone owning all the country's wealth collectively, but in practice, it doesn't trust people to make their own decisions about anything. Everyone is equal, but some (the leaders) are more equal than others.

(because their data didn't spot the new fitness trend that has caught on over the past year, which is making everyone buy bicycles instead of cars). This is how countries with command economies usually end up with **scarcity** (not enough bread) or **surplus** (too many cars), instead of having just enough for everyone (which would have happened if they had just let people decide for themselves).

The other problem with the command economy (and Communism) is that it doesn't take into account one important thing about human nature—the **power of incentives**. If everyone is going to get the same salary no matter how hard they work or how smart they are, *no one will bother working hard or being smart at all!* But if you offer people incentives (rewards)—the more kurtas you stitch, the more money you will stand to make; if you don't miss a single day at work, you will win an all-expenses paid trip to the Dubai Shopping Festival—

they will work harder, smarter and more efficiently. That is why most countries have now done away with Communist governments and command economies and gone over to democratic governments and a different economic system.

(One variant of the command economy is the **planned economy**, where the government makes a master plan for how development should go, but then allows individuals to take charge as long as they keep to the plan.)

Market economy: No rules; let's paartayyyyy!

Now imagine (sigh! your poor overworked imagination!) a country where it isn't the government, but the **market** (all the buyers and sellers in that country) that decides what crops to grow, and how much, what minerals to mine, and how much, what kinds of bread to make each day, and how many loaves of each, what medicines to produce, and how much of each to stock in which pharmacy, how much to pay someone for the work he or she does and so on. The market makes these decisions based on what people *want* to buy, not what people *should* buy. Producers don't want to make things that consumers don't want (that way, there is no surplus, or waste), and consumers are happy knowing that what they want will always be available (i.e., there is no scarcity).

The market also decides the price of each good based on the situation ('It's Diwali and people are spending like mad, so it's a good time to give discounts so they will buy more!' or 'The festive season is just over and no one is spending any money, a good time to give discounts and get rid of some extra stock.' or 'Whoa! Everyone is suddenly into organic food, time to jack up the prices on everything organic!' or 'Wow, this accountant is brilliant. I want her to work for me so bad that I will make her an offer she can't refuse. I'll pay her double what anyone else would pay her.*) The government does not interfere in any of these decisions.

Also, it is individual people, not the government, who own the means of production, which includes factories, hospitals, schools, airlines, mines, banks, electricity companies, water companies, garbage companies, and so on. And... hey, hang on a minute, you don't have to *imagine* all this. This is what things are actually like, more or less, in India, and in many other countries!

But only 'more or less', because there are problems in a pure market economy too; the kind of problems that the founders of Communism were worried about. If a country allows the market to decide everything, the market, which is essentially selfish, will only do things and produce goods that will make a profit, instead of doing things and producing goods that are necessary and good and right for the country or things that will help the poor and underprivileged and eventually build a fairer society. That

---

*In the accountant example, the price is being decided based on a person's skills, labour and time—all of which are considered 'goods' in Economics.

is why, most democratic countries, including India, have adopted a combination of command and market economies, which is called the mixed economy.

Mixed economy: A little bit of everything in my life

If you've read this far, you know that the economic system that actually makes practical sense is a mix of the two extremes. Most countries in the world today have a mixed economy, but the mix itself is different in each case. In countries like Singapore, Australia and the USA, for instance, the mix has a lot more 'market' in it than 'command' or 'planned'. Countries like Norway, Sweden, Iceland, Denmark and Finland have a different kind of mix—they are called **welfare states** because the government owns and runs all the schools, colleges, universities and hospitals in the country so that it can provide free education and healthcare to its citizens, but otherwise allows the market to decide things.

In India, we have a mix that includes some planned economy (if you've studied Five Year Plans in Civics, you know what that is about. If you haven't, go look it up!), some command (the government still entirely owns and runs some industries like weapons manufacturing, although that may also change soon), and a lot of market.

Another concept which has often worked well for India is a concept called **public-private partnership** (public means government-owned, private means owned by individuals), where the government and one or more private companies jointly own and run industries. That way, private companies are allowed to make decisions based on what the market wants and make profits for themselves, but the government gets to keep an eye and ensure that no private company is focusing so much on profit that it begins to do things that are bad for the country or the society (environmental pollution, overpricing of goods, unfair work practices, unethical behaviours that only benefit certain people, and so on).

Overall, since 1991, after India opened her economy, things have gone very well for us. Today, based on GDP or Gross Domestic Product, which is a fancy name for 'the money value of all the goods and services produced by a country in a year' (India's GDP was around 2,066 billion US Dollars in 2014), India is the seventh-largest economy in the world, and growing at a fast clip! It would grow much faster if there wasn't so much corruption, so much illiteracy, and so much poverty, but those problems will take a while to solve. The good thing is that those problems have to be solved if the country has to go forward, and so people have begun to focus on them now. The battle has begun, and you can—and should!—join it.

Bet you didn't know that!

An ancient Indian tradition = a unique kind of economy

There is another unique kind of economy that doesn't fall into any of these categories. It is called the 'gift economy'. The concept of 'selling' things does not exist in this economy (i.e. when you give someone something, you don't expect money in return). Even the concept of swapping things, or barter, does not exist. You see why this is called a 'gift economy'? If such an economy did exist, where people unselfishly gave away things to each other, do you see what a beautiful world it would be? It would be the exact opposite of a society where the selfish, greedy, profit-seeking 'market' drives everything, where money becomes more important than human relationships. But can such an economy exist, except between very close friends and family? If you think about it, we even give birthday gifts with the expectation of a birthday gift in return.

But the amazing thing about human beings is that we can, when we really want to, rise above our worst natures. To ensure that this happens, some societies create formal practices. The ancient Indian tradition of *daana* is one such. The closest English translation of *daana* is charity, although it doesn't quite have the same meaning. When you give *daana*, say the ancient scriptures, you must expect nothing in return; you are not even allowed to feel, 'Aww, what a lovely person I am! I made the giftee so happy!' The scriptures go on to say that if you want to lead a blessed life, you must, must, MUST regularly give *daana*; and you must especially give away things that you are fond of, without feelings of regret, and without hoping that now the giftee will give you something that she loves too because you were so unselfish about giving your favourite thing to her.

Sounds really difficult, huh?

But human beings are doing *daana* all the time, even though they may not realize it. Every time someone donates blood to a stranger, volunteers time at an old-age home, writes a software program and shares it on the Web for the world to use (and improve) for free, gives money to help an artiste or an innovator chase a dream via a crowdfunding* campaign, or jumps into a river to save a drowning person, they are doing *daana*. And it is precisely because of that parallel gift economy that runs quietly under the world's other economies that the world is still such a wonderful place.

P.S. It isn't only humans that behave unselfishly. Evolutionary biologists, from Darwin onwards, have found that altruistic

---

*Crowdfunding is an exciting new way of raising money from random strangers to bring good ideas to life. Let's say you want to make a movie on an amazing group of people who are transforming a village. You believe that if people saw the movie, it would make them go out and transform other villages around them. You want to offer the movie free to everyone to watch and share on the Internet. It's a great idea, and it's an idea with its heart in the right place, but you don't have the money to hire the equipment and the camerapersons and the editing studio—and you can't make the movie without these. You decide to 'crowdfund', so you put your idea up on a crowdfunding site (wishberry.in and ketto.org are two Indian ones) and ask people to donate as much money as they can afford or want to, to help you make your movie. If people believe in your idea, they will send you money, and if enough people send you money, you will be able to make your movie. No one person may have the money, time or skills to make the movie, but when a crowd of like-minded strangers come together, miracles can happen!

behaviour is quite common in the animal kingdom. Vampire bats regularly regurgitate blood and donate it to other members of their group who haven't, for one reason or another, been able to feed that night. Vervet monkeys give alarm calls to warn other monkeys—and thereby other animals—that a predator is around. Their calls draw the predator's attention to them, putting them at greater risk, but they still do it. And we all know how things work in ant and bee colonies, where truly altruistic worker ants and bees spend their entire lives building nests, foraging for food, and feeding and caring for their queen and her babies.

Yup, being unselfish could well be part of our evolutionary DNA, a 'gene' that helps the human species survive!

BIG QUESTION 3

We have millions of really poor people in our country. Why doesn't the government simply print more money so that everyone has some?

I know, right? But there are very good reasons. However, the answer is rather convoluted, and involves understanding several other things first, like why governments print money at all. So brace yourself, this is going to be a long one.

What happens when you print money? The amount of money that people have increases, but, at the same time, the price of things goes up, so that nothing actually changes. The poor can still only afford what they could before the money was printed.

Eh? How does that work?

Year 1: The government prints some extra money

Let's say there are ten people in a village. The government decides to print five 100-rupee notes and gives one note each to five people in the village (A, B, C, D and E). Suddenly, there is more money overall in the village, or in the village 'money pool', never mind that only five people have it.

A—₹100
B—₹100
C—₹100
D—₹100
E—₹100

Overall increase in the village's 'money pool'—₹500

Now let's say it is the mango season, and a lovely harvest of mangoes has just come in. The mango farmer, Alphonso, has five boxes of mangoes, and is selling them at ₹50 each. A and B arrive first, eager to spend their money.

Day 1 (morning): 1 box—₹50

That afternoon, C and D arrive to buy mangoes. Alphonso sees an opportunity! He ups the price!

Day 1 (afternoon): 1 box—₹75

That night, A's family finishes the box of mangoes. They enjoy them so much that they want more. But he cannot afford them now, because Alphonso has done it again! E buys the last box of mangoes for ₹90.

Day 2: 1 box—₹90

You see? When the amount of money in a system increases (by ₹500 in our example), without the number of goods available increasing (there are only five boxes of mangoes available), the prices of things go up. In other words, the value, or **purchasing power**, of your money goes down. ₹100 can no longer buy today what it could buy yesterday (two boxes of mangoes).

At first, A and B benefited from the extra money they received and were able to buy a box of mangoes for ₹50. They would not have been able to do so if they didn't have the extra money. But in the end, everyone lost out. Yes, even Alphonso, despite making all that extra money (he made ₹340, instead of the ₹250 he would have made had he sold his mangoes at ₹50 a box).

How? Because, when Alphonso goes out to buy bananas the next day, he will find that the price of bananas has gone up too (because A, B, C and D have decided to spend their leftover money on bananas, and the sudden demand for bananas has pushed the price of bananas up). If you extend this example to many more people suddenly coming into money and a LOT more money in the 'money pool', you can see how the prices of many other goods will also go up, in a domino effect, sending prices up as a whole. That's why it's sort of silly for governments to simply print money and give it to people. It not only doesn't help the poor, it is bad for everyone.

This kind of increase in the general level of prices of things is called **inflation**. There are many reasons that inflation occurs, but one of the reasons is 'more money in the system' (see page 92 for more details). Inflation is generally considered a bad thing because it decreases the value of the money you have.

Despite knowing how this works, governments do print more money every year. One reason is of course to replace the torn and old notes in the system, but the second is to 'keep the economy running'. Governments believe it is *necessary* to print more money every year. Why?

Year 2: The government prints no money at all

Let's consider a slight variation on our previous example. Alphonso, happy with the response to his mangoes, and having more money to spend because of the killing he made in Year 1, decides to buy another mango farm from Farmer Langra. Langra goes off to spend the money from the farm sale on bananas, sugar and clothes. The producers of bananas, sugar and clothes are happy. Many people in the village have got prosperous because of the extra ₹500 the government decided to print in Year 1.

In Year 2, Alphonso has fifteen boxes of mangoes to sell, the ten extra ones coming from his new farm. He does not know that the government does not plan on printing any money this year. What happens next?

Day 1: 1 box—₹60

Without any extra money coming into the system, no one can afford to buy mangoes at Alphonso's price.

Day 2: 1 box—₹30

Sadly, Alphonso slashes the price by half before the fruit can go bad, and manages to sell all his fifteen boxes.

Poor Alphonso! He was hoping to recover the money he spent on his new mango farm, but ended up earning only ₹90 more than last year despite selling three times the number of mangoes (fifteen boxes instead of five). Simply because no one in the village (including A, B, C, D and E) had the extra ₹60 to spend on mangoes this year (because no one gave them the extra ₹100 each, since the government didn't print any extra money).

Worried about the future, Alphonso decides not to take any more risks. Instead of buying another farm like he had planned to do, he locks up his money safely in a bank, thus taking his money out of the village's 'money pool'. That affects all the other 'producers'—the other mango farmers with farms to sell, the producers of bananas, clothes, sugar— everyone. Worried, *they* begin locking their money away too. The economy of the village stagnates. Nothing new is being produced and what is being produced is not being bought. Everyone is pessimistic and unhappy.

But suppose the government had decided to print more money this year? Suppose they had decided to print ₹600 worth of money and give ten people (instead of five) ₹60 each (instead of ₹100)? This is what would have happened.

Year 2: The government prints some extra money, a little more than last year

Day 1: 1 box—₹60

Alphonso sells ten out of fifteen boxes of mangoes, making ₹600.

Day 2: Alphonso and Raspuri have their Big Idea

To make good use of the remaining five boxes of mangoes, Alphonso and his wife Raspuri decide to make mango juice and sell it.

Day 3: The mango juice stall is up

Everyone loves Raspuri's mango juice! Excited, the couple considers setting up a more permanent juice shop.

Two months later

Raspuri rents a place in a good location and pays rent to the owner. She employs two of the ten people in the village to help her. She pays them a salary, which they may use the next year on buying mangoes from Alphonso.

Sure, all this activity will also push up prices of things a little bit and thus cause inflation, since everyone has more money. But because there are also more goods in the market—mangoes, mango juice, shops for rent—inflation doesn't matter so much. In fact, a little inflation is a good thing; it keeps the economy running.

A good economy helps producers like our farmer feel confident about the future. It encourages them to take risks by spending money to produce more goods, because they feel they can earn it back, maybe even make a profit. As for the customer, she now has more choices about where to spend her money. Everyone benefits! In a bad economy, people don't want to take risks, and the economy slows down and stagnates. Everyone loses.

Of course, governments don't go around handing freshly-minted money out to people like lollipops. They make more money available to people in other ways. They may make sure that banks have more money, so that there will be enough to lend to people who want to borrow money to start fruit-processing plants or papad-making units or software companies or car factories or hospitals or schools, or to buy homes or land to grow organic vegetables. All this borrowing and building will create products—juice, jam, pulp, papads, cars, organic vegetables—and services such as medical care, education, and software programs. It will also create employment as people have to be hired to build the factories and teach at the schools and code the software. These people will earn salaries, which they will spend on the new products. Hurray.

But all this frenetic economic activity does push up the prices of things, which is why *everything* costs more today than it did when your parents were your age, and even more than they did when your grandparents were your age. But in many ways, that's not something to whine about.

LEARN THE LINGO

Inflation

The meaning of the word 'inflation', in Economics, is 'a general overall increase in the prices of things' in a country. Most people say that 'inflation is caused because governments print more money', but some economists say that it is actually the other way around, i.e., 'governments print more money because there is inflation'. Either way, for our purposes, it is enough to know that inflation and 'more money in the money pool' go hand in hand, whichever comes first.

Now, what are some of the factors (besides governments putting more money in the money pool) that cause inflation?

▸ **I'm the bossman: this is going to cost you.** If a producer has no competition, he has **market power.** People who want what he is selling have no choice but to buy it from him. Therefore, this guy can merrily jack up his prices, causing inflation. That's what Alphonso, in our example, did in Year 1. Economists would call our farmer a monopolist, and his business a **monopoly**.

▸ **Everyone wants it, and is willing to pay the price.**
If there is a sudden increase in demand for something
which is in short supply, prices go up, causing inflation
(**demand-pull inflation**). In our example, people in the
village who suddenly found themselves flush with money
all wanted mangoes since it was the season. This was
unexpected, and the supply available could not keep up
with the demand, causing prices to zoom. (This is also
what happens to the price of tickets to an important
IPL match, although that is not entirely unexpected.)

▸ **Dude, it cost me to make this thing.** If it costs more
to produce something this year than it did last year,
then obviously the producer has to make up the extra
money he spent. So the price of the product goes up
(**cost-push inflation**).

However, inflation is never equally bad for everyone. So
who benefits, at least for a while? And who loses?

▸ The producers whose products are selling at high prices
win, their customers lose.

▸ People who have borrowed money from other people
win—because of inflation, the money they return has
gone down in value, so they are actually returning less
than they borrowed. The lenders lose.

▸ Inflation can really hurt producers in a country that has
high inflation when they trade with other countries. Let's
say Alphonso has become such a big mango merchant
that he has signed a contract with a Chinese company

to supply 100 boxes of mangoes to them every season, at ₹100 a box. He stands to gain ₹10,000 from this trade. If India has really high inflation one year (which makes the value of Indian money go down), that ₹10,000 is simply not worth as much to Alphonso as it would have been if there had been low inflation. (Low inflation would not have affected him much, because everyone expects that there will be some inflation, and charges a little higher for their goods for that reason.)

And so, the moral of the story is that, with inflation, just like with everything else in life, the Goldilocks Principle works best. Not too much, not too little, but *just* right.

What does India buy when she goes shopping?

Everyone agrees that too much inflation is a bad thing. That's why countries are paranoid about inflation numbers, and are constantly measuring and tracking them. But how do you measure inflation?

One popular method (which India also uses) is to track a number called the **CPI (Consumer Price Index)***. How is it calculated?

▸ First, statisticians study a load of data and work out what the Indian customer mainly spends her money on. Obviously, there will be some differences in what different people spend on, depending on their age, their

---

*The CPI has only recently begun to be used to calculate rate of inflation in India. The more traditional way of calculating it is the WPI, or the Wholesale Price Index.

preferences, where they live (city or village, warm place or cold place, mountains or plains), and how much money they have. Broadly, though, experts have figured out that the things most people spend on are: food and drink, clothing and footwear, housing, electricity, petrol, education, communication (phone, radio, television), personal hygiene (soap, shampoo, toothpaste, detergent), travel, medical care and recreation.

▶ All these are thrown into what is called the Indian customer's **basket of goods and services** (things like food and footwear are goods, things like electricity and education are services).

▶ Statisticians now try and work out how much Indian families spend—on average—for each of these goods and services, as a percent of their total expenses. Do they spend more money on food or on rent? Do they spend more on clothing or on education? Based on the results, they figure out what is more important and what is less important to the customer.

▸ Each of the different categories is now listed in order of importance, and a number called a weighted average is calculated for each. We don't need to go into the details of how this is calculated; all you need to know is that a higher weighted average means that that item has a higher importance for the customer than something with a lower weighted average. The figure shows the weighted averages for the Indian basket of goods. (The 'Miscellaneous' category includes travel, medicare, education, communication, personal hygiene, etc).

**THE INDIAN SPENDING CHAPATI,
AND HOW IT SLICES UP**

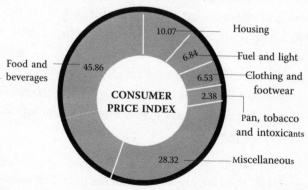

▸ Every month, the price of the overall basket is calculated. This is the CPI for that month. Has the price gone up or down compared to the previous month? If it has gone up (which means inflation has happened), by how much has it gone up? The difference in the CPI is used to calculate the **monthly rate of inflation**. At the end of the year, the monthly rate of inflation for the previous twelve months is put together and the **annual rate of inflation** is calculated. PHEW!

Over the last ten years, India's highest annual rate of inflation—15 per cent—happened in 2009 (that means, in 2009, the prices of things in our basket went up by 15 per cent. In other words, the purchasing power of our money went down by 15 per cent, which is not such a great thing). The lowest was in 2007—5.5 per cent. This, many economists feel, is an acceptable number. It's just a little over a recommended rate of inflation (4 per cent) for a growing economy, where everyone is borrowing like mad (i.e., putting more money in the money pool) to build things and grow things and make things and mine things from inside the earth, so that more people can be employed and more resources can be used well. In January 2016, we achieved the target of below 6 per cent inflation again—hurray!

Developed countries, where most of the development has already happened, have a very low rate of inflation, just a little over 1 per cent.

P.S. How do we get the data about what things cost across the country? Well, there are people who actually go around and collect this information, from some 310 towns and 1181 villages! In fact, this is one of the jobs that village postmen and women do, apart from delivering mail.

Bet you didn't know that!

The tale of the hundred trillion dollar note

Sometimes, after a country has been through war or some other disaster, when it is not possible for the government to tax people and collect revenues, it prints lots and lots of new currency to pay off all its debts and to fill its banks, so that the banks can then lend money to whoever wants it. However, since there are no new goods being produced to balance all the new money entering the system, the value of the money falls rapidly, leading to inflation. When inflation increases very rapidly, at a rate greater than 50 per cent a month, the country has what is called **hyperinflation**, which is a nightmare.

Zimbabwe experienced the hyper-est form of hyperinflation in November 2008, when the rate of inflation was—hold your breath—7.96 BILLION per cent! That means a loaf of bread which cost, say, 1 Zimbabwean dollar (ZWD) in the year 2000, cost 7.96 billion ZWD in November 2008! Over the years, the government had printed currency notes of larger and larger denominations, so that people could at least carry enough money in their pockets to buy their groceries*. On 16 January 2009, the Reserve Bank of Zimbabwe issued the largest denomination ZWD ever— the 100 trillion dollar note! What could it buy? Not even the tiniest bar of chocolate!

In June 2015, Zimbabwe started 'phasing out'—or doing

---

*Imagine if this had happened in India, where our largest denomination currency note is ₹2000. You'd have to take a barrow-full of notes to buy a loaf of bread!

away with—its official currency. The government asked people to bring all their ZWDs—in wheelbarrows or trucks or whatever—to the banks and exchange them for US Dollars (USD). How many ZWDs would people have to give in to get 1 USD in return? Just 250 trillion.

If you ever come across one of those 100 trillion dollar notes though, hang on to it. It is now a collector's item, and is selling at around 200 USD on eBay.

BIG QUESTION 4

How come one Indian rupee is only worth about 1.4 US cents? Who's the guy who decides this stuff? And can I write him a strongly-worded letter?

Hmmm. Your indignation is admirable, but unfortunately, India's poor **dollar exchange rate** (the need to pay out more and more rupees in return for fewer and fewer dollars) is not decided by any one guy that you can write a letter of complaint to. Instead, like karma, it is a result of our own past and present actions. The good thing is, there is nothing permanent about this—the exchange rate is fluid, it changes every day, and, if we do things right, the exchange rate can get better.

One thing you must know before we go any further is that the exchange rate is not some absolute number. That means, if we say that the exchange rate is 68 rupees to the USD, it doesn't mean that it is also 68 rupees to the pound or 68 rupees to the yen. Exchange rate is relative; you can only have an exchange rate between any *two* currencies, and it changes according to *which* two currencies you are comparing.

Also, a country's dollar exchange rate (its exchange rate against the USD) is a very important number because it indicates how 'healthy' a country is economically. More countries will trade with countries that are in good economic health, and that will help that country's economy get even healthier.

The country with the stronger currency and better exchange rate (let's call it Desh) is usually at an advantage, because it spends less of its money to buy things from the other country (Videsh). Poor Videsh, on the other hand, loses out—it has to spend *more* of its money to buy things from Desh. That's why governments fret so much about the exchange rate.

So what affects this mysterious, quicksilver, ever-changing dollar exchange rate? Many things, and even smart economists with tons of experience often find it difficult to explain them all in a way that everyone can understand. Let's just look at some of the important (plus easy to understand) factors here, using India and the US as examples, although these would work with any two countries.

When does the rupee get 'weaker' against the dollar (i.e., when does India's dollar exchange rate get worse)?

▶ **When India has more inflation than the US.** Inflation, as we figured out in a previous section, basically ends up reducing the value of your money—it can buy less than it used to. So higher inflation is bad for your exchange rate.

▶ **When India spends more money buying things from the US than selling things to it.** Let's say India spends ₹1000 on buying American goods and earns only ₹900 by selling Indian goods to America. India will now have a **trade deficit** of ₹1000–₹900 = ₹100. A high trade deficit brings down the value of the rupee against the dollar.

▶ **When India becomes a country in debt**. Let's say India has a high trade deficit, and therefore has less money to spend. So it borrows money from other countries. As its debt gets higher, other countries become reluctant to lend money to India, for obvious reasons. (If you knew that your friend had borrowed ₹50 each from your classmates A, B and C over the past year and has not yet returned their money, you will think twice before lending him another ₹50 yourself.) Now that it has become difficult to borrow money from other countries, India may decide to simply print more money to cover its deficit, and we know that printing excess money without the goods to back it leads to inflation. The more the inflation, the worse your exchange rate. It's a vicious, vicious cycle.

When does the rupee get stronger against the dollar?

▸ **When more countries would rather lend money to India than to the US.** See, countries very rarely have enough money to do everything they want to. So they are always looking to borrow money from other countries. Now, the countries that can lend money have only a limited amount of money to lend, so they have to decide which country to lend it to. Obviously, they will pick a country in which their money will grow faster, i.e., a country that offers a higher rate of interest on their investment*. So one way for a country to get more countries to invest in it (lend to it) is to offer a higher rate of interest on their money.

▸ **When the price of the Indian goods that the US is buying goes up faster than the price of the American goods that India is buying**.

▸ **When India's government is stable** (no civil wars, no military coups, no dictatorships, regularly-held free and fair elections), **and its economy is growing steadily each year** (more food being grown, more goods being

---

*If you've studied Simple Interest at school, you know that Amount = Principal + Interest; that is, the amount (A) that you pay back to the lender is the sum of the amount you borrowed (P) plus the simple interest (I), where I = P * rate of interest * time. Clearly, when the rate of interest is higher, I is higher too. So countries would prefer to lend to a country that offers a higher rate of interest, so that they get more money back.

produced, more services being offered), the US (and other countries) will pick India to lend money to over countries whose governments aren't so stable or whose economy isn't growing as steadily. That will help India gain a favourable exchange rate.

Yup, it's a long, winding and uphill road to a better exchange rate, but everyone wants it and is working towards it, one rupee at a time.

Bet you didn't know that!

A McDonald's burger not only impacts your health, but your country's too!

The price of a Big Mac burger in your country as compared to another country can tell you how strong your currency is against that country's! There is actually a semi-serious thing called the **Big Mac Index** that the *Economist* magazine came up with in 1986. But before we get to that, let's rewind a little.

Remember we spoke earlier about GDP, or Gross Domestic Product (see page 78)? GDP is a measure of how poor or rich a country is. One way of calculating a country's GDP is by finding out the combined value of all the goods and services produced in that country over a certain time period, say a year. GDP calculated by this method is called **nominal GDP.** A country with a higher GDP is considered 'richer' than a country with a lower one.

But there are problems with this method. Since each country's GDP is calculated in its own currency, how do you compare the GDPs of two countries, say India and the

US? You do this by converting both their GDPs into some other common currency, usually the US Dollar. How do you convert? By using India's dollar exchange rate. Let's say USD 1 = INR 65.

But we know that India's dollar exchange rate is largely based on the exports and imports between India and the US (see points 3, 4 and 5 in the previous question). Surely, said economists, the relative richness or poorness of India when compared to the US, and the strength of the rupee compared to the dollar, cannot depend so much on India's trade with the US. A better way, they felt, would be to figure out how the lives of people in India and the US compared to each others' in money terms—how much did people in each country get paid for similar work, what could each afford to buy with the money they got paid, did they each have a similar variety of different products available in their countries, and so on.

So economists came up with another way to compare the relative wealth of two countries (India and the US in our example), and the relative strengths of their currencies. Here's what they did. First, they put together a 'basket of goods' that people in the US regularly use (1 litre of milk. 1 loaf of white bread, 1 kilo of rice, 1 litre of petrol, rent of a single-bedroom apartment, a bus/taxi ride inside a city, a pair of Levi's jeans, a pair of Nike shoes, a combo meal at McDonald's* and so on) and calculated the total cost

---

*They couldn't use the Big Mac in this particular basket because the Big Mac is a beef burger and McDonald's doesn't serve beef in India!

of the things in that basket in US Dollars. Then they put together a similar basket of goods in India, and calculated the total cost of the basket in rupees. Then they created a new 'dollar exchange rate' based on the difference between the two costs. This new exchange rate gave a better sense of what ₹100 would buy in India compared to $100 in the US, i.e., how 'powerful' ₹100 was compared to $100, in their respective countries.

This kind of exchange rate, based on the purchasing power of a currency, is called **purchasing power parity.** A country's GDP calculated using this method is called that country's **PPP GDP** (phew, so many letters!). Although this kind of calculation is not perfect either, many economists feel it is a better measure of the strength of a currency than nominal GDP.

Here's a question for you: Do you think the rupee would have a better exchange rate against the dollar if we used PPP to measure it? You can find out through an experiment. Put together your own basket of goods, and find out what each of the things in that basket costs in New York, and what it costs in Mumbai. Then calculate the PPP exchange rate for the two baskets and see!

Let's help you get started. A loaf of white bread in New York City costs about $3 while it costs about ₹30 in Mumbai. In other words, $3 is equivalent in value to ₹30. How many rupees is $1 equivalent to then? Dividing both by 3, we find that it is equivalent to (or can buy the same amount of bread as) ₹10! But according to the regular dollar exchange rate, $1 is equal to ₹65! See what happened when we used

PPP to compare currencies? The Indian rupee suddenly got six times stronger against the dollar!* No wonder India is the world's seventh-largest economy by nominal GDP but the third-largest by PPP GDP.

*P.S.: Some countries believe that GDP itself is not a good way to measure the wealth of a nation. India's neighbour, Bhutan, for instance, has a different measure, called **GNH or Gross National Happiness***! It believes that how happy its citizens are is a better measure of a country's wealth than anything else. A British organisation called the New Economic Foundation has come up with another index called the **Happy Planet Index**, which measures how well a country has taken care of its environment while providing for its citizens. Another popular one is the **Human Development Index,** which measures things like education level and life expectancy of a country's citizens along with its GDP.*

You can come up with your own economic index to measure a country's wealth. Like the MDD (Masala Dosa Deliciousness) Index, the MYTVD (Most Yelling On TV Debates) Index, the CSHOMYWARTIL (Crazy Stuff Happening Outside My Window Any Random Time I Look) Index.
India will be World No. 1, hands down, on all three!

---

*If you check out the Big Mac Index for July 2016—http://www.economist.com/content/big-mac-index—you find that the price of the Big Mac equivalent in India, the Maharaja Mac, is around ₹160, while the price of a Big Mac in the US is around $5. In other words, $5 and ₹160 are equivalent on the Big Mac Index, which means $1 is equivalent to ₹32, not ₹65, at least as far as Big Macs are concerned. Which is different again from the loaf of bread equivalence. Because each item in the basket of goods will give you a different dollar-rupee equivalence, only the TOTAL costs of the baskets are compared to give a more accurate PPP.

WHAT YOU AND I THINK ABOUT WHEN WE THINK ABOUT ECONOMICS (A.K.A. MICROECONOMICS)

The ancient Greek mathematician, physicist, inventor, engineer and astronomer Archimedes—the same guy who ran through the streets naked, screaming 'Eureka!'—once boasted, 'Give me a lever long enough and a fulcrum on which to place it and I shall move the world.' Archimedes, who did not invent the lever but was the first to explain how it worked, was of course talking about an actual lever, like a crowbar. And however unlikely it seems that one man can move the earth, scientists agree that it can be done, given the right conditions.

Economics has levers too (even though they look nothing like crowbars). And unlikely as it may seem, it is individual men and women, who make small buying decisions with their limited amounts of money, who actually influence the demand for goods, the supply of goods, and the prices of goods in the global market, and operate the levers that keep the economies of their countries, and the world, running. Or not. Yup, as an individual consumer, you have that kind of superpower!

In fact, your actions are so important to economists that they created an entire branch of Economics just to study them. That branch of study is called Microeconomics.

Here are four questions—and answers—that will introduce you to the kinds of things economists talk about when they talk about Microeconomics.

BIG QUESTION 1

I am thinking of setting up a lemonade stall at the Holi mela in the park near my house. What price should I sell each glass for?

So your mum hasn't said that you should just give it away for free, because trying to make money out of people is somehow a bad thing? Great, you have a mum who thinks exactly like the market! Here's what the market says: Whatever has gone into the production of your good (in your case, lemonade)—raw materials, time, labour and skills—it is only fair that you should get an amount of money in return that is equal to their combined value.

But how in heck do you put a 'money value' on time and effort and skills? By extension, how is the right price of *anything*, including a glass of lemonade, determined?

The answer to that is quite complex, even bordering on the mystical. Even economists find it difficult to explain these things well. But there has never been a shortage of theories.

A price for everything and everything at a price

What actually decides how much a thing* costs? Here are some theories that people have played around with.

Theory 1. It depends on how much work has gone into producing the thing.

One of the first theories about how a good should be priced was the **Labour Theory of Value**, which was floated around

---

*The 'thing' could be a good or a service; we will limit our discussion here to goods.

the time that our friend Adam Smith was writing his famous book. It said that the price of something was a measure of how much work had gone into making it.

Let's say, that at your Holi carnival, you put a bunch of lemons, some sugar and salt, a jug of water, a knife and a long-handled spoon on a table in your stall and called it 'Lemonade (with some assembly required)—₹10 a glass'. We're betting it won't be the hottest seller at the mela. However, if you made the lemonade yourself and set it out in a jug, with plenty of ice and a few sprigs of mint floating in it, people will actually pay ₹10 for a glass. What has added value to your offering? The fact that you put in some work—labour—to make it. This is what the Labour Theory of Value said, anyway.

But is the price *only* based on how much work went into something? Consider this. Let's say you have a competitor, A. Rival, who also has a lemonade stand on the other side of the mela. A. Rival used some super-efficient lemon-squeezing device, and a mixie to powder the sugar, and therefore got her one jug of lemonade made in fifteen minutes, while you spent forty-five minutes squeezing lemons by hand, hand-pounding the sugar, and going to the store to get a bunch of mint leaves to float in your pitcher. If the amount of work (and time) that went into producing something decided its price, your lemonade should sell for ₹30 while hers sells only for ₹10. Try that pricing and see what happens. Most likely, A. Rival will sell out while you sit around swatting flies.

Yeah, so, no go. Still, the Labour Theory of Value stuck around for almost a hundred years, because it is (still) true that labour is definitely one part of what determines the price of something.

Theory 2. It depends on the 'intrinsic value' of the thing.

Some economists believed that everything has an 'intrinsic value', a value that it has simply by being itself. That, they said, would decide what its price would be. But is that true? If nobody wanted to buy gold, would its intrinsic value— that of being a shiny metal imprisoned in rock—count for anything? Coming at it from another angle, would you say a bitter powder made by roasting and crushing little brown seeds had much 'intrinsic value'? And yet, people all over the world pay a lot of good money for coffee! So the theory of 'intrinsic value' is basically bunk.

Theory 3. It depends on how rare (or common) the thing is.

Could it be that something is more expensive because it is rare, while something else is cheaper because there is plenty of it? That is somewhat true, but it is also true that people would be unlikely to pay money for something *just* because it is rare. If you were selling your (quite terrible) kindergarten art projects—they are very rare!—at your stall instead of lemonade, do you think people would be queuing up to buy them? What if you were selling pangolin poop? See?

Theory 4. It depends on how much money the greedy manufacturer wants to make with the thing.

So basically, the manufacturer decides a random price and the hapless, held-to-ransom customer coughs it up if he wants the thing. Right. Here's a suggestion: why don't you try it and see if it works? Fix a random price, say ₹75, for a glass of lemonade, and see how many people (besides your grandmom) step up and buy a glass. We would guess zero. The thing is, customers are (a) not stupid; and (b) do not have limitless amounts of money to spend.

Yeah. None of these theories were quite satisfactory. So economists were forced to come up with a new one, which has served us well so far.

It is called the **Law of Supply and Demand**, and it believes that it is the 'market' that decides the 'right' price of something. According to this law, there are four factors involved in the decision.

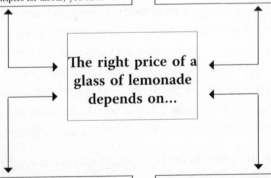

The supply, or how much lemonade you are selling—which will depend on (a) how much you think people will want to buy (b) how much time and energy you have for the task, and (c) how much capital (money for ingredients, space for production, helpers for labour) you have.

The demand, or how much lemonade people want to buy—If there are only going to be around 25 people at the mela, it is unlikely that they will buy more than 35 glasses between them—even on a hot day, and especially if you have a competitor.

The right price of a glass of lemonade depends on...

The quantity, or how much lemonade is available—based on supply (how much you made based on your constraints, *plus* how much lemonade is available at you competitor's stall) and demand (how much you think customers will want).

The 'perceived value' of lemonade, or what people are *willing* to pay for a glass—how much of it is available (the more there is, the less it will be valued) and how badly they want it (how hot is it today? how good is your lemonade?).

These four factors push and pull each other in all directions, until the movement settles at the 'right' price. But the right price is not fixed. It changes with time and circumstances because of many reasons. The price of your lemonade, for instance, may go up because:

▸ The cost of raw materials (lemons and sugar) goes up.
▸ The cost of production goes up, i.e., you are now in Grade 10 and you have less time for melas, so you have to make an extra effort to have the lemonade ready.
▸ The demand for it goes up because there is less of it available (maybe your competitor ditched lemonade and moved to sugarcane juice, which got spoilt in the heat, sending everyone to your stall).

Similarly, the price may go down because of a variety of reasons.

The 'perceived value' of a good also changes with circumstances, which in turn affects the price. At the Holi mela, with your competitor, A. Rival, also selling lemonade, customers may only be willing to pay ₹10 a glass, which makes ₹10 the 'right' price. But let's say these customers are lost in the Thar Desert (with a full wallet to boot!) one afternoon in May, and you are the only lemonade stall in sight (which makes you a **monopoly**, see page 119). In that situation, these very same customers may be willing to pay as much as ₹500 a glass (you extortionist, you!) because your lemonade is now perceived as a 'lifesaving drink' rather than 'a nice way to encourage a young entrepreneur'.

So basically, according to the Law of Supply and

Demand, the market will eventually 'settle' at the right price, under the circumstances, whatever they may be.

That's all very well, But can you trust the market to settle at a fair price? Let's see.

Situation 1: Holi Mela

You have sold out your stock of lemonade (two jugs, or 20 glasses, @ ₹10 a glass), hurray! You have made ₹200 in all. People came back for more, but you were all out (because you didn't anticipate demand correctly). Your competitor, A. Rival, also sold out her stock of lemonade, although the verdict was that your lemonade was much better than hers.

Lessons learnt:

▶ Your lemonade sells, and so does A. Rival's.
▶ You must make more lemonade next time.
▶ You must charge more than A. Rival, since people feel that yours is better.

Situation 2: Independence Day Mela

Brimful of confidence, you make four jugs of lemonade (40 glasses), and price it at ₹25 a glass this time. A. Rival has four jugs too, but she is charging only ₹15 a glass. Because everyone agrees that your lemonade is better, a few customers come to you even though you are charging more (the 'perceived value' of your lemonade is higher). But many decide they would rather spend the extra 10 rupees on something else, and go to her stall instead. She sells out, making ₹600. You sell only 15 glasses, and make only ₹375. Plus you're left with 2.5 jugs of lemonade that no one wants.

Lessons learnt:

▸ A. Rival knows that her lemonade is not as good as yours, so she will always price it a little lower, knowing that there will always be many people who won't want to spend more than ₹15 a glass.

▸ You know that your lemonade is better, and there will always be a few people willing to pay a little more for it, but not too much more.

▸ Both of you know that you underpriced your lemonade at Holi.

Situation 3: Diwali Mela

A. Rival makes four jugs as usual, and sells it at ₹15 a glass (the formula that worked for her). You make three jugs this time, and sell at ₹20 a glass. This time, however, A. Rival is only able to sell 33 glasses (because there are people who don't mind paying ₹5 more for a better glass of lemonade, and so buy from you instead), and makes ₹495 (33 glasses @ ₹15), while you are able to sell 25 glasses, and make ₹500. Both of you have some stock left (because you can never predict demand too accurately).

Lessons learnt:

▸ A. Rival made less money than she did last time, which means your pricing was more on the mark this time.

▸ You actually made *more* money by *reducing* the price of your good. (Aaaah! That's why stores so often have those seemingly ridiculous 'Flat 70 per cent off' sales!).

▸ Between A. Rival and you, you made sure the customers

at the mela were kept really happy—each customer got what he wanted, at a price he was willing to pay, and there was more lemonade (of both kinds) available in case he had wanted another helping.

▶ It took a couple of tries to get it right, but by Diwali, A. Rival and you have figured out how much of your goods to stock, and the consumers are happy that they have a choice.

▶ You know what's the coolest part, though? It happened by itself, as if by magic, by invisible, untraceable signals that your customers and you sent to each other through your actions. That's what they mean when they say *the market decides the right price of a good*!

P.S.: At the Christmas mela, A. Rival and you use the brilliant 'Diwali Formula' again and set out your lemonade stands. But this time both of you sell only HALF of what you sold at Diwali and make a big loss! What happened? Someone set up a tomato soup stall at the far end and took all your customers! Because seriously, who wants iced lemonade on a cold December night when there's hot soup available?

LEARN THE LINGO

Price Elasticity

How often do you buy a new notebook, priced currently at say, ₹20, for school? How often would you buy it if its price went up to ₹25? ₹30? ₹35? If you said 'I would buy it just as often as I buy it now' to all three questions, it means that the price of the notebook would never affect your need (or demand) for it. Whatever they are priced at, you cannot do without school notebooks, so you will just continue to buy them. Economists would say that 'the demand for school notebook is completely **price inelastic**'. In other words, your need for notebooks, and your willingness to buy them, does not change with their price.

Think about something a lot more expensive, and relatively unnecessary, like a pair of Nike sneakers. If the price of a pair of Nikes went up from ₹2000 to ₹3500 (the same percentage increase as the notebook, when it went up from ₹20 to ₹35), you would probably look around in the market to see what other brands of sneakers cost (unless you have very indulgent parents!). Your demand for sneakers doesn't change, but your demand for *Nike sneakers* has changed because of the steep price hike. Economists would say that your demand for Nike sneakers is **price elastic** or that it changes with the price.

Generally speaking, this is how price elasticity should work. The demand for essential goods (rice, onions, milk, petrol) are more or less price inelastic, while the demand for luxury goods (gold jewellery, cars, houses) and goods which have decent substitutes, are price elastic. If what you are planning to buy is price elastic, you will either simply postpone buying it (in case of a luxury good) until prices fall; or you will buy the cheaper substitute instead (like in our sneakers example).

But this doesn't always happen. There are certain goods which go against the **price-elasticity-of-demand (PED)** logic. One of them is telecom services. Today, telecom services—mobile phone services, broadband services and so on—are considered an essential good. But demand for them is price elastic i.e., the demand for them rises sharply when the price declines, and declines when the price increases. The other good that bucks the PED logic is the demand for ultra-luxury goods, like fine wines, designer handbags and fancy cars, which actually *increases* as their price increases (making those goods price inelastic), because of various factors, including:

▶ **The Snob Effect:** Your status goes up if you have those things, so you don't mind splurging on them.

▶ **The Bandwagon Effect:** Just because more people are buying a particular brand, other people begin to think it's reliable/better quality/cool, and buy it, even if it is more expensive than other brands.

▶ **The Network Effect:** More people today buy (more expensive) smartphones rather than dumb phones, because you can only be on WhatsApp if you have a smartphone, and your entire 'network' of friends, family, plumber, boss is on WhatsApp, and you will lose out if you are not.

▶ **The Reverse Effect:** People would rather buy more expensive goods than cheaper ones because they believe, for no logical reason but simply because of a 'feeling', that something that is cheap must be of lower quality than something that is more expensive.

Phew! Mind games everywhere!

A short note on markets—Monopoly, Oligopoly, Monospony

In a true 'competitive market' like your apartment's Diwali mela, where manufacturers are free to charge what they want and customers have a choice (two lemonade stalls), the market eventually settles at the 'right price'. But not all markets are free and competitive, and in such markets, things could go very wrong. Here are some examples of non-competitive markets.

Monopoly: The customer isn't king. I am!

A monopoly situation happens when there is only one producer of a good in the market. How does this come to pass? Let's say this producer was so rich that he could sell his good for way less than the 'right price' because he was in no hurry to start earning a profit. Other producers of the same good could not sell so low and therefore lost all their customers. Eventually, they shut down their factories, leaving only the rich guy in the market. Now that he has monopoly, i.e., no competition, this guy decides to price his good way *higher* than the right price. Customers are now forced to buy the good at this high price if they want it, because no one else is selling it.

Monopolies are created in other ways too. Sometimes, governments themselves become monopolies. The Indian Railways, for instance, is a monopoly. Unlike taxi services, which anyone can run, no one but the Indian government can offer railway services from one place to another. So whatever the state of the trains or the stations, or whatever price a train ticket costs, everyone simply has to put up with it.

Sometimes, it is just circumstance that creates a monopoly—like you and your lemonade stand in the Thar Desert in May.

Oligopoly: Let's keep this between ourselves.

An oligopoly is somewhat like a monopoly, except that instead of just one producer, there are a limited number of producers of a good. Or there are several producers, but only two or three of them have most of the 'market share', i.e., most of the customers.

Are oligopolies good for the customer? Yes and no. Let's say there are only three producers. On the one hand, each of them has to be careful not to raise prices too much above the right price because customers will then just go to the other two. Also, none of them can sell an inferior quality good, because if he does, his customers will go to the other two. In both these cases, the customer benefits. But there is also the possibility that these three producers will sit together (forming what is called a **cartel***) and jointly decide a price for their good which is higher than the right price. This is great for them, because they will make a lot more money than they would have otherwise, but the customer will again be in a monopoly situation of 'no choice', and be forced to cough up the high price if she wants the good.

For instance, in the Independence Day mela, if there were no other cold drink stalls around, and you and A. Rival had jointly decided that she would charge no less than ₹20 a glass and you would charge no less than ₹25 (for your better quality lemonade), any customer who wanted a cold drink would have been forced to pay at least ₹20 a glass. You would have made more money than you deserved, simply by 'cartelising' in an oligopoly situation. The customer would have been fooled into believing she had a choice, when in reality she was being looted.

---

*The best-known example of a cartel is OPEC, the Organisation of Petroleum Exporting Countries. Here's the short back-story of OPEC. In the 1950s, the world oil market was controlled by a group of seven oil companies, most of them American, called the Seven Sisters. They owned oilfields in Middle Eastern countries like Iran, Iraq, Kuwait and Saudi Arabia, and would buy oil from them at whatever price they (the Seven Sisters) decided. If any country refused to sell at that price, they would stop trading with them, putting that country into deep financial trouble.

In 1960, Iran, Iraq, Kuwait, Saudi Arabia and Venezuela came together to form OPEC. They decided that it would be OPEC, and not the Seven Sisters, who would decide the price of a barrel of oil. The Seven Sisters would be forced to pay it, because they needed the oil! By forming a cartel, the oil-producing countries had neatly turned the tables on the foreign oil companies!

Monospony: The customer is queen.

Here's where the tables are turned. There is only one customer and many producers, all of whom want her money. In this reverse monopoly situation, the customer is truly queen. She can decide what price she will pay for a good, confident that one producer or another will agree to provide it at that price rather than losing her custom.

As you can see, this is equally bad for the market. If the customer dictates the terms, the producers will not even make as much money as they spent on making the good or providing the service, and will eventually stop making it, which is eventually bad for the customer, too.

Monopsonies are not a fantasy. They actually exist. Let's say a coal mining company sets up shop in a remote forested area. People who live in the villages around have hardly any source of employment. They tend their small fields, collect firewood and honey from the forests, and sell them at a faraway town. The new coal mine promises a steady job, and more money than they can hope to make otherwise. Therefore, everyone wants to work in the mine. This is a monopsony situation—there is only one customer (the owner of the coal mine) and several producers (the villagers) who want to sell their good (in this case, their labour) to him. Since the customer is all powerful in this situation, he can pay the villagers very little, way below what he would have paid in a non-monopsony situation and still have enough labour for his mine.

As you can see, none of these three situations— monopoly, oligopoly, monopsony—is a good thing. To make sure they don't happen, governments have all kinds of rules and regulations in place. But governments also have to be careful—too many rules upset producers, who will then be reluctant to put their money into manufacturing goods, but too few rules harm consumers. Yup, it isn't easy being the government!

BIG QUESTION 2

Guess what! The Residents' Welfare Association of our locality cancelled the Holi mela this year! Apparently, someone (who didn't even attend the mela, by the way!) complained that there was too much litter in the park after the previous mela. And someone else complained that the music disturbed his son, who was preparing for his Grade 12 exams. But that's just not fair to us producers, is it?

Yeahhh. It's terrible how unfair it all is to you. Not! What is unfair is how often producers and consumers of a good do not realize how their actions affect the silent bystander, who is not even involved in what's going on but has to suffer the consequences of those actions. In the case of the mela, everyone inside was thinking of their own benefit—you and every other producer was only thinking of how to sell his product and make as much money as possible, and every consumer was only thinking of how her money could be spent so that she got maximum value out of it. Neither was thinking of the impact of their actions on people and things *outside* of themselves.

Economists call this kind of impact an **externality**. If the impact is not a favourable one for the bystander, like in the case of the people who complained about the mela, it is called a **negative externality**.

What if the impact is favourable? Let's say an NGO raised money (you didn't contribute) and cleaned up the filthy lake next door. Instantly, the stink that used to fill your house every time you opened your windows disappeared, and without you lifting a finger. You have just benefited from a **positive externality**. Or let's say your parents decided that you should be vaccinated against chicken pox, even though it was not a compulsory vaccine like the polio vaccine or the DPT one. This is a positive externality for the friends you hang out with—they now have a smaller chance of getting chicken pox themselves, since you are protected against it!

In the case of the mela, the bystander suffered a 'cost' (an afternoon of noise, a messy park) because of your actions; in the second (the lake clean-up), the bystander (you) gained an unexpected 'benefit' (hurray! no more stinky house!) from someone else's actions; in the third, the bystander (your friend) benefited from your responsible action of getting yourself vaccinated.

You see how the actual 'cost' of something is not really its price? The price of a good (see previous section) is decided by 'market forces' like supply, demand, quantity and perceived value, but it doesn't take into consideration the good and bad impacts (or costs) of the making, selling and using of that good. But that cost is very real. In the case of the mela, the organizer lost the ability to host the next mela—and make a ton of money—at that park, because of the negative externalities caused by the first one!

What are the most common 'negative externalities'?

▸ **Air pollution**: Car manufacturers and users may not often think about this, but the air pollution their machines are responsible for causes severe health problems for the bystander and the environment.

▸ **Smoking:** It causes health issues to bystanders who simply inhale the smoke.

▸ **Open garbage dumps:** One of India's biggest and ugliest problems, which not only spread disease but also impact tourism. Who wants to go on holiday to a filthy, stinky country?

▸ **Unrecyclable plastic bags:** They choke lakes and drains and cattle intestines.

▶ **Pollution of lakes and tanks:** Toxic, untreated sewage that impacts aquatic life-forms in terrible ways and endangers human and animal lives around it (while the factory bosses, who live elsewhere, are not affected).

What can be done to minimise negative externalities?

Governments do a bunch of things—they make laws, impose fines on factories that pollute and stores that hand out plastic carry bags to customers, levy 'green taxes' on vehicles*, ban smoking in public places, organize door-to-door garbage collection so that no one has a reason to dump their garbage on the street, and so on.

But none of us needs to wait for the government to do these things. Just being mindful of our actions can minimise negative externalities both for ourselves and for everyone else.

For instance, if the Mela Organizer (MO) had thought about the negative externalities his event was likely to cause, he could have taken steps to keep them to a minimum. He could have:

▶ Ensured that the music was played at a low volume, with the speakers turned away from the houses around.
▶ Hired a cleaning crew to pick up litter through the day, so that the mela 'left no trace' by the next morning. Never mind the bystanders, even visitors to the mela

---

*In Delhi, for instance, where air pollution has reached seriously hazardous levels, trucks passing through the city have to pay a pretty heavy 'green tax' since November 2015. The Delhi government hopes that because of the high tax, many trucks will stop taking the short cut through the city and instead go around the city to get to their destination, thus reducing the air pollution in Delhi.

would have had a better overall experience if the place had been clean.

▸ Placed big bright litter bins all over, so that more litter went into them than on the ground.

But of course, it isn't only about being mindful. Cleaning crews and litter bins cost money, and where is the money to come from? It would only be a foolish and short-sighted MO, however, who would ask such a question. A smart one would realize that it is actually in his own best interest to ensure that negative externalities are kept to a minimum. He would figure out creative ways to raise money for the cleaning crews from the mela customers themselves.

Here is one idea that we came up with for our MO.

He could charge stall owners a 'Clean Mela Fee', and use that to pay the cleaners. Of course, as a good stall owner, you would have whined and complained about the extra charge, but the smart MO would appeal to your greedy, selfish, profiteering heart with convincing arguments. He would remind you that more customers are likely to visit a clean, litter-free mela. He would tell you that a clean place, like cool weather or a scenic landscape, makes people feel a sense of well-being. Happy people, he would go on to say, are likely to hang around longer, and spend money more easily, than people who are uncomfortable in their surroundings. By this time, you are begging him to accept your Clean Mela Fee.

Can you think of any other ideas for our MO?

Now, you've gone and paid up your Clean Mela Fee, but as a sharp entrepreneur, you want to recover that money from your customers. After all, it is the customers who are doing the littering (which is why your MO is hiring a cleaning crew in the first place). It is also customers who are benefiting from the clean environment that you are creating. Surely, they should pony up a little too! Ummm, okay, but it is you who is making a profit at the end of the day, not them.

Still, if you think that you will be more motivated to participate in the mela if there is a chance you can recover your 'Clean Mela Fee', there are ways to do it.

Here are a couple of ideas.

IDEA 1

Price each glass of lemonade a couple of rupees higher than you were going to, and hope that customers will still buy your lemonade at the higher price.

IDEA 2

Put a donation box and point people towards it gently. This way, you keep customer contribution voluntary, and make them feel good about themselves (when they contribute) and warm towards you.

Bet you can think of several more yourself!

Either way, you ensure that everyone involved in the mela—organisers, producers, consumers—do their bit towards making sure that no one is made to suffer through their actions.

In the end, really, good Economics is all about good manners, and concern for other people and the environment. If you think about how you can do business so *everyone* wins and not just you, it is very likely that your business will do very well indeed. Plus you will have the satisfaction of being a 'socially and environmentally responsible entrepreneur'. What's not to like about that?

LEARN THE LINGO

The Tragedy of the Commons

In 1833, English economist William Forster Lloyd wrote a little pamphlet about the problem of overgrazing on the 'commons' in England. 'Commons' was another word for the pasture that was open to every cattle-herder in a village to graze his animals on. The pamphlet was titled 'The Tragedy of the Commons'. Lloyd said that since the pasture belonged to everyone (and therefore to no one), the selfish ones among the herders would graze their cattle to the maximum, until eventually the pasture itself would get depleted and be of no use to anyone.

Today, we use the word 'commons' to mean any shared resource—the cookie jar at home ('Mom, Bhaiya finished my share of the cookies too!'), the overhead water tank in your apartment complex ('I bet that awful lady in 6E who is always having houseguests used up all the water. I'm going to complain to the association!'), a neighbourhood park ('The mela people littered it so much I can't even go there for

my morning walk. Next year, no permission for the mela!'),
or the air in a city ('Those people driving around in their
big cars ruin the air for all of us!').

As you can see, the problem remains the same. If no
one is supervising how much of the commons each person
uses, or how each person uses it, it is human nature to
either take more out of it for yourself (especially when no
one is looking!), or use it in a way that only benefits you,
until the commons is either depleted (cookies finish) or
becomes unusable (park gets too full of litter).

What is the solution? In large communities, like cities
and countries, the government acts as regulator and
policeman, deciding who can use a shared resource (the
commons), how much each person (or corporation) can use
it, and in what manner each person (or corporation) uses
it. In India, for instance, you need to have licences (which
the government issues) for activities that involve extraction
of non-renewable resources, like coal mining and drilling
for petrol. Some countries like China even regulated (until
recently) how many children a couple could have (one).
They were trying to control their population, because a
larger population would cause 'overgrazing' on the country's
'commons', or its shared resources.

In smaller communities, however (like an apartment
complex, or a neighbourhood), where everyone can sit
together and talk about things, the community itself can
regulate the 'grazing'—everyone realizes that losing the
resource is bad for all of them, so they figure out a way to
work things out among themselves to make sure the sharing

is fair. In our cookie jar example, you and your brother may decide to split the cookies amongst yourselves right at the beginning and not filch from the common jar, because a fight over cookie sharing only leads to Mom refusing to bake any more cookies for a month, no matter who ate whose share. Which is bad news for both of you.

BIG QUESTION 3

My mom says that whenever I take part in a mela again, I should serve my lemonade only in reusable glasses, not in disposables. That will not only reduce the litter my stall creates, it will also be better for the environment. I agree in principle, but I also know that many people prefer disposables because they feel it is more hygienic. What if no one buys my lemonade because I am using reusable glasses?

Excuse me, is this even an Economics question? Actually, erm, yes. Doesn't it belong in a book on the environment?* Weirdly enough, while it could certainly be in that book, it is definitely not out of place here. A new branch of Economics called **Behavioural Economics** is now all the rage, and it explores how human psychology impacts how and where people spend their money.

Human beings are generally rational. You will see very few people burning a currency note, for instance. But we

---

*Read the other book in this series *So You Want to Know About the Environment* by Bijal Vachharajani.

often also behave in highly unpredictable and irrational ways. Our behaviour when we are in a group (while watching a T20 cricket match in a stadium, say) is very different from our behaviour when we are alone (like when we are watching the match at home). This irrational, unpredictable behaviour influences how we make decisions about what to buy, too.

We are guided by:

▶ **Our emotions.** 'This is a great product at the right price, but I don't like the woman who runs the store, so I will not buy it.'

▶ **Our moral conditioning.** 'This is cheap, so who cares if it was made using child labour? I'll buy it!' or 'This is a great product, but it uses too much water. I will not buy it.'

▶ **Social pressure.** 'This phone is perfect for my needs and so well-priced, but will my friends think I'm cheap if I buy this over the more expensive one?' (see 'Snob Effect', page 118)

Manufacturers—and governments*—will lose their customers if they don't think about all these factors before they start selling their products. As a manufacturer of lemonade who wants to make as big a profit as possible while being responsible about the environment, so should you.

Let's list out the points you should consider while thinking of your particular problem.

---

*In the case of governments, the 'customers' are the citizens who have the power to vote for or against them, and the 'products' are ideas such as equality, justice, development.

▸ You know very clearly which side you are on. You think disposables are bad for the environment, and you don't want to be responsible for adding more disposables to the already overflowing landfill outside your town through your actions.

▸ You want to make a profit. What's the point of being an entrepreneur if you don't make a profit?

▸ A lot of your customers are going to have some problems with reusables, for the following reasons:

  • They will worry about hygiene (what if the glasses haven't been washed well after the last person used them?).

  • They may want the convenience of picking up their drink from your stall and then walking around the mela sipping on it, which they cannot do if the lemonade comes in a glass which has to be returned. And so on.

But here's the thing. In their hearts, most of your customers *also* want to do the right thing. They do care about the environment—many of them are probably carrying cloth bags with them for their mela shopping—and they will support a young entrepreneur who is using reusables.

Remember, though, that they are more likely to support you *if it is convenient to do so* and if there is *something in it for them*. Economists refer to this 'something in it for them' as an **incentive**. If you want to influence your customers' **buying behaviour** (i.e., make sure they buy your product), you should give them 'incentives'.

Incentives need not be related to money. You don't have to sell your lemonade at half the cost to push them to buy it (if you do, human psychology will kick in again and they will probably think that you are selling it cheap because there is something wrong with it!). Although money incentives work—otherwise stores would not be having those fabulous sales—psychological incentives often work even better. You could, perhaps:

▸ **Name your product cleverly**, so that it induces curiosity and draws customers. Like, say, 'Litter-free Lemonade', or 'Garbage-hatin' Lemonade'.

▸ **Appeal to customer hearts, not heads.** Gently nudge customers to buy your product over others with  posters that evoke nostalgia ('Your Naani doesn't serve her nimbu paani in plastic cups and neither do we!') or guilt (A visual of a dustbin full of used paper-plastic cups from fast food places and roadside coffee tea places, with the line 'How many trees did you destroy last week?') or good old awww ('Show the planet some love—drink our lemonade!').

▸ **Address your customers' concerns.** Make sure your glasses are sparkling. Have someone in a clean apron wiping off freshly washed glasses in the stall, with a clean cloth. Make sure your surfaces and counters are wiped down regularly. Stand the clean glasses upside down on cheerful and clean teacloths. Make customers forget their hygiene argument.

▸ **Make things convenient**. Have a couple of friends and family with 'Garbage-hatin' Guys and Gals' sandwich boards walking around the mela with empty trays. Tell your customers they can hand in their used glasses to them once they are done. Destroy the 'but I don't want to come back all the way here to return my glass' argument.

▸ **Create one killer incentive**. Make badges— 'I did my bit for Swacch Bharat today'— and pin them to every customer's sleeve. Your customers will love it. Everyone will know how virtuous they've been without them having to say anything. What's in it for you? Other people will ask your customers about the badges, and word about your lemonade will spread.

Honestly, wouldn't *you* buy lemonade that sells itself this way? See, it isn't all that difficult to be a responsible entrepreneur *and* make a profit in the bargain. Do it!

Bet you didn't know that!

The seat-belt rule actually causes more accidents!

'Provide the right incentive, and you can tweak customer behaviour' is a mantra that most economists believe staunchly in. But even well-meaning, well-thought-out incentives can sometimes have very unexpected outcomes. In his best-selling book *The Armchair Economist*, American economist Steven E. Landsburg offers data showing how seat-belts and airbags, both of which are meant to protect people inside a car, often end up causing more accidents, if not more deaths! He explains this apparently contrary phenomenon using behavioural economics. When they know their ride is safer, he says, drivers take more risks, and drive more recklessly. If you find that difficult to believe, says Landsburg, think about the opposite: do people drive more carefully when they think they are more at risk? Of course they do! The opposite is true too. Simple!

Consider another example. In the recent past, instead of paying their CEOs (Chief Executive Officer, or the Big Boss of a company) a fixed salary, some companies have started paying them a variable salary. Part of the salary is fixed, but the other part depends on how well the company does that year. If the company makes a profit of, say, ₹10,000, the CEO gets to keep, say, 5 per cent of it (₹500), since it was under his leadership that the company did so well. This was meant as an incentive to keep the CEO working hard and thinking creatively, because the company's profits were linked to his own. The thinking was that with a fixed salary, the CEO wouldn't care so much how the company did, since he was assured of getting his fat pay cheque at the end of the month.

Now companies are rethinking this again, because what actually happened with the variable salary was that dishonest CEOs began showing false profits! If the company had made a profit of ₹10,000, they would fudge the accounts and show it as ₹20,000, so that they got to take home

₹1000 extra instead of only ₹500. The incentive backfired! Of course, that doesn't mean that incentives don't work. They do, although it may not be in the way that you think they will, or want them to.

Just as an exercise, think about the incentives people offer you to change your behaviour. (Remember not all incentives are 'positive' ones. For instance, fear of punishment is a big 'incentive', and very popular with all figures of authority—governments, schools, parents.) Do all the incentives you are offered work the way they are supposed to? Are positive incentives more effective in your case than negative ones, or is it the other way around? Do you work harder at your studies if your parents promise you a reward for doing so, or if they threaten to take your TV rights away?

Think about the incentives governments offer. Is Singapore so clean only because there is such a stiff penalty for littering? Do you think there should be such a penalty in India too? What about a penalty for peeing and spitting in public? Would it work? More importantly, would it be fair to impose such a penalty without first having enough dustbins/public toilets in place for people to use?

BIG QUESTION 4

My dad tells me that I should put all the profits from my lemonade stall into a savings account in a bank. Should I? He also says the bank will not only keep my money safe but will, a year later, give me more money than I put in.

That's weird. Shouldn't I be paying the bank for keeping my money safe?

You have a wise dad. And that is a good question. But before we answer it, let's talk about banks a little. What is a bank, anyway? It is a 'financial institution' that essentially has one main function—lending money to anyone that wants to borrow it. Banks and individual money-lenders of one kind or another have existed since ancient times; some of the first mentions of a simple money-lending system, as far back as 3500 years ago, come from India's Vedic texts. But the word 'bank' dates back only to the fourteenth century when the Renaissance was sweeping across Italy. Money-lenders in Florence used to sit at *bancas* (Italian for 'table') covered with green tablecloths, dispensing loans to people.*

Why would anyone lend his hard-earned money to someone else? Out of the goodness of his heart, to bail out a fellow human in trouble? One would wish that people were so kind, but classical Economics tells us that it is mainly selfish impulses that make people do the things they do. So why do people lend money? In other words, what's in it for the lender? The answer is: a lot of money!

You see, when the borrower returns the amount he borrowed to the lender, he also pays him a 'borrowing fee' (called 'interest'). This fee is the money-lender's income, what he gets to keep for himself. Essentially, therefore, a bank or a money-lender is earning money without doing

---

*Most money-lenders in Italy were also Jewish. Now you know where Shakespeare got his inspiration for Shylock in *The Merchant of Venice*.

any work at all. In fact, many people see **usury,** which is the fancy word for the practice of charging a borrowing fee, as a way for the lender to take advantage of the borrower's misfortune when instead he could have lent him the money for nothing.

This was precisely the reason that many ancient and medieval cultures, and religions like Christianity and Islam, prohibited usury for several centuries. People who practised usury were hated and looked down upon as greedy loan sharks, feeding off the blood of people in need. Even today, Muslim law considers usury a sin, and Islamic banks do not charge interest on loans. The rest of the world, however, has made its peace with having to pay interest to banks on borrowed money. The good part is that the interest rule applies to banks as well. When they borrow money, they have to pay it back with interest too.

But how does that make sense? Why would banks need to borrow money? They already have all the money they need, don't they? Actually, no. There is only a limited amount of money in the system, and banks need to borrow money too, if they want to have enough to lend to someone else. Banks borrow mainly from the central bank (in India, this is the Reserve Bank of India), and from—hold your breath— *you*! Yup, the money you put in your savings account is actually money that you are *lending* to the bank! So of course they have to pay you a borrowing fee, which is why your money 'grows' when you put it in a bank.

But if banks are lending and borrowing all the time, and paying out the interest they collect from their borrowers to their lenders, how do banks make any money at all? A-ha! They've worked that one out nicely. They simply charge a higher borrowing fee from borrowers than they give to lenders! In other words, a bank's **lending interest rate** is always higher than its **borrowing interest rate.**

Let's see how this works.

You borrow ₹1000 from your bank. The bank charges you a 'borrowing fee', or a 'lending interest rate' of 10 per cent per year. That means, when you return the money to the bank a year later, you will have to pay:

1000 + 10% of 1000 = 1000 + 100 = ₹1100.

At the same time that you were borrowing from the bank, your sister was lending a similar amount to the bank, by depositing ₹1000 in her bank account. The 'borrowing fee' that your sister can charge the bank (or the 'borrowing interest rate') is fixed, and is, let's say, 8 per cent. When the bank pays back her money a year later, she will get:

1000 + 8% of 1000 = 1000 + 80 = ₹1080

You see? When you borrow ₹1000 from the bank, you have to pay them ₹1100 after a year, but when they borrow the same amount from you, they only have to pay you ₹1,080 after a year. The difference (1100–1080 = ₹20) is the bank's income, the money they get to keep for themselves.*

---

*This is also the way that foreign exchange (forex) firms make their money. They sell you foreign currency at a higher exchange rate than they buy your foreign currency from you. If you are travelling to the US and need to exchange your INR (Indian National Rupee) for USD (US Dollars), you have to pay about INR 69 for 1 USD. If you want to reconvert your extra USD to INR after you are back, the forex guy will only pay you around INR 66 for 1 USD. The ₹3 difference per USD is his income.

Twenty rupees may seem like a small amount, and really not worth the bank's while to do all the work involved in earning it. But remember that banks do not lend and borrow just a few hundreds of rupees, they lend and borrow hundreds of crores of rupees, so the difference between the money they pay out (to lenders) and the money they earn (from borrowers) is ginormous. That makes it very worth it for them!

Who wants to be a millionaire?

In fact, the longer you keep your money in the bank, the more it grows, because of a useful trick called compounding. Also, the younger you are when you start putting money in a bank account, the more you stand to gain. Here's how compounding works.

Let's say you start earning a salary at the age of twenty-three. Each month, you take ₹1000 out of your salary and put it in a piggy bank. At the end of one year, you put the ₹12,000 you have saved into a bank account and forget about it.

Let's say the bank is paying you 8 per cent interest every year. At the end of Year 1 after you put the ₹12,000 in, your money has grown to:

12,000+ 8% of 12,000 = 12,000 + 960 = 12,960

The next year's interest is calculated on *this* number, not on your original deposit. This is called compounding*. So, at the end of Year 2, your money has grown to:

12,960 + 8% of 12,960 = 12,960 + 1036 = 13,996

By the time you are thirty-three, at the end of Year 10,

---

*You've probably studied Compound Interest in math by now. This is the same thing.

your money has more than doubled, to ₹25,907. By the time you are forty-three, it has grown to over ₹55,000. And by the time you are fifty, your ₹12,000 has grown to close to a lakh, without you lifting a finger.

Now consider this. If, instead of putting aside ₹1000 a month from your salary, you put aside ₹2000, and, at the end of the year, deposited ₹24,000 in the bank as your initial deposit. What would this amount to at the end of Year 10? Almost ₹52,000. By the end of Year 20, it would be around ₹1,18,000. And by the time you are fifty, it would have grown to almost ₹2 lakh!

Remember that we are only talking about the money you put aside that *one* year, the year you were twenty-three. If you put aside a similar amount (₹12,000) every year for the next ten years, you will have almost ₹2 lakh in the bank by the time you are thirty-three, not fifty! It's like magic!

Now imagine if you started putting your savings in a bank when you were only fifteen. Do you have rupee signs dancing in front of your eyes? Good. Now stop imagining and go put your money in that bank already!

Bet you didn't know that!
Banks work out of big fancy buildings for a reason!

Here's an interesting bit of trivia: How come big banks are always located in the largest, fanciest offices, in the most expensive part of town? Because they have tons of money, that's why! Well, yes, but do they really need those big, fancy buildings? Wouldn't they rather use the money they earn somewhere else?

Well, like everyone else, banks use behavioural economics

as well.

Like every other vendor in the market, banks are trying to get your money. But unlike most other vendors, they don't have a real 'product' that you can touch and feel. So what are they *actually* trying to sell to you? What do they want you to buy? The product that banks are selling to you is an idea called 'trust'. You will only 'buy' from them (i.e., give them your money) if you trust them. You wouldn't lend money to someone you didn't trust, would you?

And banks have figured out that big, impressive buildings send a telepathic message out to people that the bank is old and solid and trustworthy! That's why they do it!

LEARN THE LINGO

A Run on the Bank!

If every single person who had a savings account in a bank decided to withdraw all her money on the same day, would the bank be able to give it to her? More importantly, what would happen to the bank if every lender demanded her money back at the same time?

The short answers to the two questions are: (1) eventually, maybe, but not immediately, and (2) the bank would have a real problem.

See, banks don't take your money and simply lock it up somewhere safe. If that was what banks did, you could very well do it yourself at home. Your money would just sit there in a triple-locked trunk, and unless some good fairy managed to magically get in and add to it, there would be exactly the same amount of money in there each time you checked, whether you checked after one year or ten.

What banks actually do is take your money and lend it to other people. As long as things are going as per usual—people the bank has lent money to are repaying their loans on time, and people who they have borrowed from are not all asking for their money back at the same time—the bank is fine. But sometimes, things go wrong. Borrowers lose their money because of a bad decision, or a natural calamity, or a political upheaval, like a war. They are unable to pay the bank back, ever. Their loans are said to have gone bad.

If a large number of big loans go bad, the bank is in serious trouble. It does not have enough money to pay back its own loans to its lenders, who are people like us! If word gets around that the bank's loans have gone bad, people will want to take their money out as quickly as possible, before the bank runs out of the money it still has. People rush to the bank. When other people hear of it, they rush to withdraw their money, too. Panic spreads as people lose trust in the bank. A bank run, or a run on the bank, is now underway!*

In real life, however, bank runs rarely happen. For one thing, even if a bank is failing because of bad loans, the public never gets to know. Often, the failing bank quickly

---

*Read Ruskin Bond's lovely short story 'The Boy Who Broke The Bank' on a bank run in a small Indian village to understand how human psychology and Economics go together.

borrows money from other banks, or the central bank of the country, and keeps things running as before, while it decides what to do. Or it shifts all its customers to another bank which has enough money to keep things running without causing any problems to the customer.

In India, particularly, bank runs have almost never happened because the government has strict rules about how much of their money banks can lend out to people. This means Indian banks always have a decent amount of money in reserve for situations where a lot of people may want to withdraw all their money. This is a good thing for customers, but not such a great thing for banks, because it limits the amount of money they can invest, and therefore the amount of money they can make for themselves. There are also rules about who Indian banks can lend to—they have to ensure that lendees can pay their loans back before they lend to them. Better safe than sorry, what? This is a good thing for banks, because it leads to fewer bad loans, but not such a great thing for customers, who have to prove their 'credit-worthiness', or their ability to pay a loan back, before they can get that loan.

Also, most Indian banks are nationalised, or backed by the government. Even if a bank 'collapses' because of bad financial decisions, the government guarantees that it will pay every penny of every lender's money back to him. That's very reassuring, don't you think? That's the other big reason why there have been almost no runs on Indian banks.

Bet you didn't know that!

Banks can create money out of nothing!

It's true! This is how it works.

Say you deposit ₹100 in your bank account. We already know that banks don't just salt your money away in their vaults; they will lend/loan it out to someone else because that's how they make money.

Now, in most countries, including India, banks are not allowed to lend out all the money that they receive as deposits. They are obliged to keep a **fraction** of it with them in 'liquid' form (i.e., as actual hard cash). This is the bank's **reserve** money. That way, if a lender decides one day that he wants all of his money back, the bank will be able to give it to him immediately*. This practice is called **Fractional Reserve Banking (FRB)**, and is the most common form of banking in the world. What fraction of its deposits a bank is supposed to keep with it is decided by the central bank of the country. (Rules like these are necessary. Otherwise, banks would be tempted to lend out all the money they borrow from us, so that they can maximise the money they make for themselves. And if some of the bigger loans then went bad, the bank—and us—would be in very big trouble indeed.)

Say the banking rules of your country insist that the bank hold at least 10 per cent of a lender's money in reserve at

---

*Of course, if every lender decides to draw out all his money on the same day, the bank will not be able to oblige (see section 'A Run On The Bank'). But because every bank has thousands of depositors, this situation (of everyone wanting their money at the same time) will almost never arise.

all times. So, if someone comes asking the bank for a loan, the bank can lend her no more than ₹90 of your ₹100. Now that person takes the ₹90 and deposits it in her bank. Her bank has to keep ₹9 of that in reserve before it lends her money out to another person. This is what the chain of transactions could look like.

You deposit	₹100	Your bank holds 10% and loans Person A	₹90
Person A deposits	₹90	Her bank holds 10% and loans Person B	₹81
Person B deposits	₹81	His bank holds 10% and loans Person C	₹72.90
Person C deposits	₹72.90	Her bank holds 10% and loans Person D	₹65.61
Person D deposits	₹65.61	His bank holds 10% and loans Person E	₹59.05
Person E deposits	₹59.05	His bank holds 10% and loans Person F	₹53.14
Person F deposits	₹53.14	Her bank holds 10% and loans Person G	₹47.82

And so on.

Do you see what has happened in the bargain, though? The bank has created money out of nothing! Here's how. You, and Persons A, B, C, D, E, F and G *think* you have ₹100, ₹90, ₹81 and so on respectively, because your bank says you do. If you go to your bank and ask for your money back, the bank will actually also give it back to you. In total, therefore, adding everyone's money up, there is apparently ₹569.52 in the system.

But. The only actual amount of money available is *your*

₹100, which you lent to your bank right at the beginning! The other ₹469.52 is entirely fictional!

Does that mean banks are cheating us? Not really. After all, they will give you the exact amount you put in anytime you ask for it, and with interest. So what's happening here? By 'creating money' through this process of using fractional reserves, bankers have worked a sort of magic across centuries. What happens to the 'fictional' money that is lent out to Persons B, C, D, E, F and G? It doesn't lie around in safe lockers, either. It is out there helping people buy machinery, build things, set up stores, build homes for themselves. All this activity generates employment for people and profits for businesses. By putting more money in the system, FRB leads to an expansion in business activity. The economy of the country grows, and that's a good thing.

The idea of FRB has its roots in the theories of a famous British economist called John Maynard Keynes. His breakout book, *The General Theory of Employment, Interest and Money*, was published in 1936.

In it, Keynes said that while it was good to allow people to manufacture, buy, grow and sell what they like without government interference, the government had to step in sometimes to keep the economy growing, especially in times when businesses failed and people lost jobs. People without jobs, said Keynes, would not spend money to buy things that other people made. That would force the people who make things to close down their businesses, because of which more people would lose jobs. This would go on and on until there would be no more money circulating, and the economy would stagnate. To prevent this from happening, said Keynes, the government and/or the central bank should step in when businesses failed, and put money into the system to create jobs and restore people's confidence, thus getting them to start spending their money again.

FRB is one banking practice that puts money into the system. However, many people (including many economists) don't agree with Keynes' Economics, and argue that there is something unethical in the way FRB works to 'create money out of nothing'. But since there are so few easy alternatives to FRB, and since it has been part of the global banking system for a very long time, it will be difficult to change it anytime in the near future.

EPILOGUE

MONEY CAN BUY YOU ANYTHING—BUT SHOULD IT?

It has been almost 250 years since Adam Smith put out the revolutionary theory that free markets and free trade— people trading with each other furiously and continuously— was the way to build wealth for everyone. He was so persuasive in his arguments and made so much sense at the time that everyone adopted his ideas, and have been doing little else than trading with each other since then. Since Economics believes that any trade that benefits both sides in some way is a 'good trade' that should be encouraged, the world today has a new God of All Things, and its name is 'The Market'.

Clearly, free trade has been good for the world. It has made people and countries super-productive and richer than they might have been otherwise. But is there such a thing as too much free trade? Are all trades that benefit both sides really 'good'? Should money be able to buy anything?

Consider these scenarios.

Scenario 1. You don't want to go and stand in a long line for movie tickets for the latest superhero movie, so you decide to buy tickets online. You know that the already expensive multiplex ticket will cost you a little more because of the 'convenience charge' that the website will tack on, but you are willing to pay it. The movie theatre is happy that it is selling tickets without having a long, noisy line forming in front of its ticket windows, the website is happy that it made money by facilitating the trade between you and the movie theatre, you are happy because of the time and effort you saved by not having to stand in line. Economists would call it a good trade.

Scenario 2. In an effort to reduce the use of plastic, your city has recently banned stores from giving out free plastic bags to customers; henceforth, there will be a charge on all bags that the store hands out. You keep forgetting to bring your own bag but don't care too much—the bag charge is small and you don't mind paying for it. The city is happy that it is making some money off your forgetfulness, the store is happy that they can still keep you as their customer (which they may not have been able to if they couldn't give out plastic bags at all), and you are happy with the convenience. Again, a good trade, according to economists.

Scenario 3. You work really hard in your Grade 12 and get a good rank in the JEE exams for the IITs. With your rank, there is a very good chance that you will get into a good engineering stream in one of them. That year, though, the government decides that they are spending too much money to fund the IITs. They tell the IITs that they must raise at least 50 per cent of their own funds to run the institute. The IITs decide that they will reserve a section of the seats—say 40 per cent—to students who want the seat so badly that they are willing to pay 5 lakh a year in fees. There is still a cutoff—you should still have a good rank—but you don't have to have a top rank. The rupees five-lakh seats quickly fill up. The institute is happy that they have raised a good sum of money for themselves, the students who got those seats are happy that they got in despite getting lower ranks. A good trade! Never mind that there are now fewer seats open to students like you who cannot or don't want to pay the high fee.

Scenario 4. You have been ill with high fever for three days. Your blood test results come back with a dengue diagnosis. Your platelets are not dangerously low yet but your parents are taking no chances. They rush you to the hospital. There are patients ahead of you in line whose platelet counts are way less than yours. But you want to get to the doctor quickly. You know that the hospital offers the option of cutting the line to anyone who can pay three times the specialist's consultation fee. Your parents pay it. You get seen by the doctor and get hospitalised immediately. You find out later that you got the last available bed. The doctor is happy that he got a higher consultation fee—he has been working his feet off with the dengue epidemic and he feels he deserves it. The hospital is happy that they got in some extra income—they get to keep a part of the doctor's higher fees—and that they filled up all their beds. You and your parents are relieved that you got the last bed and were treated by the best doctor available.

Now, since everyone involved in each of the four trades

in the four scenarios ended up happy, economists and The Market would call all four 'good trades'. But are they all really good? Also, are they all equally good?

Scenario 1 is probably fine. Someone who didn't want to pay the convenience charge but wants to see the movie will just get to the ticket counter earlier and get her ticket. If the movie is sold out by the time she gets to the head of the queue, too bad. She will come back the next day.

Scenario 2 is not as fine as the first. Sure, you don't mind paying for your plastic bag, but the point of the government's effort is to reduce the use of plastic. If people like you can't be bothered to remember to bring their own bags and instead keep paying for plastic and using it anyway, the landfills (and gutters and cows' stomachs) are still going to be full of it. Anything that contributes to that surely cannot be a good trade.

Scenario 3 is even worse. You are nodding vigorously, because you are feeling the pinch this time from the 40 per cent reservation of seats. (Keep in mind that this kind of 'reservation' is different from the other kind, where seats are reserved for students from economically-backward or socially-oppressed sections of society. The first kind favours the rich, the second favours the disadvantaged. You decide which is fairer.) Sure, this particular trade ended up with all parties involved being happy, but what about the parties that suffered because of it, even though they were not directly involved?

Also, what then happens to the value of the good being

traded, which in this case is the IIT seat? Earlier, just getting a seat in an IIT would win the student huge respect; now the student will have to specify that he got an IIT seat 'on merit' to win the same respect. And people will still wonder if he is telling the truth. You see? The seat itself has been 'devalued'.

Scenario 4, you will agree, certainly cannot be called a 'good trade'. Sure, you ended up getting the best and quickest treatment because such a system existed in the hospital (for now, let's assume it is a purely fictional system which doesn't actually exist in real life), but just for a minute, put yourself in the shoes of someone else in the queue who had waited in line since morning, was worse off than you health-wise, and was next in line to see the doctor before you burst onto the scene. Not such a 'good' trade now, is it?

American political philosopher Michael J. Sandel thought about such trades a lot. Then he put down all his thoughts in a fascinating book called *What Money Cannot Buy*.

Sandel argues that we should be careful about allowing The Market, and 'market values'—which say trade is good, period—to dominate our lives in areas where such values have no place. He argues that markets should have 'moral limits'—we should not only think about whether a trade is 'good', we should also think about whether a trade is 'fair' to everyone around, even those not directly involved in the trade itself.

While it is generally okay for a trade to favour the rich— pay more money for a better seat on a plane or a bigger room in a hotel—it is not always okay when it comes into areas where other values should matter. In some areas of community life, the questions we should be asking are not 'Can you pay for it?' but 'Do you deserve it?' , 'Do you need it more than someone else?', 'Were you here first?' and 'Will making this trade hurt someone else?' Yup, the same kinds of questions you should ask yourself before you do or say things in your non-trading life, too.

Only when we all ask such questions will we be able to create not only a more productive and prosperous world, but also one that is fairer, gentler, more ethical, and a better place to live in for all of us.

ACKNOWLEDGEMENTS

A big thank you to:

- Dr Raghuram Rajan, former governor of the Reserve Bank of India, who actually responded, within the hour, while he was still RBI governor, to a cold-call email sent to his @rbigovernor.in address, saying he would not mind taking a look at the manuscript of this book. Within the next ten days, he had done so, and even sent in a warm endorsement of it. Which goes to prove, yet again, that the busiest, most talented people are often the nicest, most efficient ones too.

- Devangshu Datta, Consulting Editor, *Business Standard*, and overall supernerd (as a schoolboy, he won the Bournvita Quiz no less than three times; as an adult, he co-wrote Vishwanathan Anand's autobiography *My Life in Chess* with him), for very kindly agreeing to read the manuscript. The only two of his many valuable suggestions that have not been incorporated are the ones about leaving chocolate (he is allergic to it) and mangoes (he hates them) out of the book.

- Mahesh Yagnaraman, alternative energy entrepreneur, self-confessed Economics passionista, and dear friend, for taking time out of his insane 'start-up-founder schedule' to read and critique the manuscript.

• Sudeshna Shome Ghosh, lovely and calm editor and friend, for not batting an eyelid when, after enthusiastically picking Economics out of a bunch of different subjects that she had lined up as possible themes for books, I confessed cheerfully that I did not know the first thing about it.